Praise for Take

'A much-needed manual, mixing inspiration, wisdom and practical tips. *Take the Lead* is a vital book for any of us seeking to advance our careers, with courage and creativity – and without losing sight of ourselves and our values.' ISABEL BERWICK, FINANCIAL TIMES

'In its concise yet deeply inspiring pages, this book offers invaluable guidance. It's a treasure trove of wisdom curated from exceptional leaders, generously sharing their insights gleaned from remarkable leadership journeys. *Take the Lead* is a delightful, effortless journey through valuable lessons, making it an essential and enjoyable read for anyone seeking to thrive in both life and career.' CLARE MAHON, MANAGING DIRECTOR EMEA, ASSOCIATION OF EXECUTIVE SEARCH AND LEADERSHIP CONSULTANTS

'Reading *Take the Lead* is like having a support team of women leaders alongside you, sharing their wisdom and experience, and fostering courage and confidence in you on your leadership journey.' KIM MORGAN MCC, CEO AND FOUNDER, BAREFOOT COACHING

'A remarkable ode to women's empowerment, and it could not be more relevant today. This book is a call to action, an invitation to dare, an encouragement for change.' JEAN-PAUL AGON, CHAIRMAN AND FORMER CEO, L'ORÉAL

'A beacon of inspiration for female leaders in the business world. Backed by rigorous research and insights from women leaders on six continents, this book offers practical advice to succeed in uncertain circumstances through creativity and self-reflection.

Take the Lead equips you with the tools to innovate, seize opportunities and ascend the corporate ladder with confidence. An invaluable guide for aspiring leaders.' HUBERT JOLY, FORMER CHAIR AND CEO OF BEST BUY, SENIOR LECTURER AT HARVARD BUSINESS SCHOOL, AND AUTHOR OF *THE HEART OF BUSINESS*

'Provide readers with a framework for innovation, change and courageous leadership. Drawing on experiences from successful leaders across the world, the authors challenge assumptions and offer a new approach to addressing the benefits of gender diverse leadership.' SOUMITRA DUTTA, DEAN, SAÏD BUSINESS SCHOOL, UNIVERSITY OF OXFORD

'The stories shared provide a great resource for leaders of any gender. The book emphasizes the benefits of creativity and innovation in problem-solving, both of which are essential skills for any leader addressing complexity.' JOY BURNFORD, CEO AND FOUNDER, ENCOMPASS EQUALITY AND AUTHOR OF *DON'T FIX WOMEN*

'A necessary and timely international take on what companies and individuals can do to close the gender gap. Featuring inspiring portraits of great female role models and clear action plans, I highly recommend this book.' ELEANOR MILLS, FOUNDER AND EDITOR-IN-CHIEF, NOON

Take the Lead

How women leaders are driving success through innovation

Anne-Valérie Corboz

Shaheena Janjuha-Jivraj

Delphine Mourot-Haxaire

KoganPage

Publisher's note
Every possible effort has been made to ensure that the information contained in this book is accurate at the time of going to press, and the publishers and authors cannot accept responsibility for any errors or omissions, however caused. No responsibility for loss or damage occasioned to any person acting, or refraining from action, as a result of the material in this publication can be accepted by the editor, the publisher or the authors.

First published in Great Britain and the United States in 2024 by Kogan Page Limited

2nd Floor, 45 Gee Street	8 W 38th Street, Suite 902	4737/23 Ansari Road
London	New York, NY 10018	Daryaganj
EC1V 3RS	USA	New Delhi 110002
United Kingdom		India
www.koganpage.com		

Kogan Page books are printed on paper from sustainable forests.

ISBNs
Hardback   978 1 3986 1414 7
Paperback 978 1 3986 1412 3
Ebook   978 1 3986 1413 0

British Library Cataloguing-in-Publication Data
A CIP record for this book is available from the British Library.

Library of Congress Control Number
2023951104

Typeset by Hong Kong FIVE Workshop, Hong Kong
Print production managed by Jellyfish
Printed and bound by CPI Group (UK) Ltd, Croydon CR0 4YY

To the women who chose to be on this journey with us,
to those who are to come, and to everyone who inspired us
to be the leaders we are.

CONTENTS

Introduction **1**

01 Creativity **17**

02 Compass **49**

03 Courage **71**

04 Connections **107**

05 Championing **131**

06 Curating your team **151**

07 Career **177**

Conclusion **199**

References **209**

Acknowledgements **215**

Index **219**

Introduction

Take the lead

Why did you pick up this book? Is it down to luck that you are now reading this book and deciding what you can glean from us? We decided to write this book because we wanted to challenge the ideas behind how women pursue their careers. While luck always plays a part, we have to decide how we use our luck, how we overcome unlucky events and how we can actively increase our opportunities for success. We wanted to start from a position of strength, the value of innovative thinking and creativity that emerges with diverse leadership.

The discussions around women's leadership have flourished across regions and sectors, with an increasing recognition that women benefit from training and development that is targeted towards their needs and context. The narrative on women in the workplace recognizes the value of diversity to provide innovative solutions for the complex problems we face. Despite the huge strides in policy and cultures around gender diversity, there is greater disparity in the workplace faced by women. Over the last decade we have produced more research and data to provide clarity on what creates barriers for women and on effective interventions that support women. However, as more regions across the world aim to address the gender gap in the workplace, there is a need to revisit the tools for women and reposition what women need and can take with them, irrespective of where they work and live.

We decided to write this book because the data presents a mixed bag. There are great strides ahead, but not at the pace of change we expect, and, of course, we are seeing a regression in some areas. Consider the summer of 2023 as we write this book; we have witnessed the most successful Women's World Cup, where players were paid for their participation in the tournament, the first female director to achieve revenues of $1 billion for a movie, and the first female astronaut from Saudi Arabia as part of the team that launched into orbit for the International Space Station. However, it's also been the summer that acknowledged the two-year anniversary of banning the education of girls in Afghanistan, the resignation of Alison Rose, one of the most powerful female CEOs in the banking industry in the United Kingdom, and the forced kiss of the Spanish footballer after their World Cup victory. Clearly, there is still work to be done.

Today we have more women in leadership positions, but we also have high attrition rates – for example, in the US in 2022, more women left corporate America than in any other period. Data from the Women's Economic Forum predicts that it will now take 135 years to reach gender parity, an increase from 99 years predicted in 2020. At this pace of change, it will take five generations to reach parity, longer than we have to solve the climate crisis. The irony is not lost on us, but with decades of experience working on women's leadership, the journey is challenging. Working in the field of women's leadership is like navigating a boat on a long journey. You set off on the journey knowing where you want to reach, but along the way the calm blue waters are replaced by turbulent storms and strong winds that can set you off track, and at times even push you back before you re-steer to move forward.

As we delivered women's leadership programmes to women from all over the world in three locations – London, Paris and Qatar – we identified similar trends. Despite socio-economic and cultural differences, the women we met experienced similar blockers: systemic institutional barriers, biases and stereotypes from their managers and colleagues, and inconsistent support to help navigate their own internal voices of doubt undermining their confidence. Addressing each of these barriers and navigating a leadership path require creative solutions in organizations that are not yet ready to address these areas.

This book presents a global perspective on the skills and tools women need to develop and choose the career they desire. The book tackles stereotypes and labels that were introduced to provide an understanding of barriers facing women, but have in turn created additional obstacles for gender equity at work. Drawing on decades of research and interviews with women from different sectors and regions across the world, the book explains how women apply tools in different cultural contexts to help navigate their careers.

Propelling your leadership career forward means working on different things, at times simultaneously, and it can be overwhelming to know where to start or what to focus on. With this in mind, we initially created a **canvas** and evolved this concept into a **boat**. Your career leadership journey is likely to be very similar to the broader women's leadership journey. Navigating your leadership career is not straightforward, there is a lot to juggle, and it's easy to make the mistake of focusing too much on one area while neglecting other opportunities.

Your career is like a boat, and how you steer it will help you navigate successfully to your leadership goals. We are very clear that there are different aspects you need to work on, not all at the same time, but building a successful leadership career requires planning and attention. If not – then what happens? Luck – maybe. It certainly has a part to play. In fact, the three of us began this journey together reflecting on how often women ascribed their career success to luck.

While there is no doubt about the benefits of being in the right place at the right time, creating a successful career is the result of tenacity, taking on stretch roles and building confidence in your abilities, particularly when facing uncertain situations. Luck matters, but, as one of the women we interviewed said, your leadership success is a combined result of luck and preparation to create opportunities. As the French chemist Louis Pasteur famously said 'Chance favours the prepared mind.'

We conducted research with one thousand women from across the world on their leadership development. We found that the idea of luck takes on an important role, as it has a positive impact on important resources for women's careers. For example, we found it positively impacted the perceived strength of women's connections and their mental agility for work. What was perhaps more surprising was the strength of connection between luck and leadership status. We found that the perception of luck was far more pertinent for women in the C-suite compared to women in less senior positions. It seems women are more likely to attribute senior leadership to some degree of luck compared to women in the early stages of their careers. This could be for a variety of reasons: perhaps women still grapple with imposter syndrome and are not quite convinced they deserve the leadership position they hold. This finding could also be attributed to the benefit of hindsight and being able to reflect on one's career path and determine when opportunities were serendipitous and, with the right skills and attitude, open for exploitation. The idea of luck is highly emotive and, in our experience, opens many conversations – we will dip into this area again later in the book.

Talking about opportunities, how did this book come about? While we all work for HEC Paris, we are spread in different locations – Paris, Qatar and London. Each of us has a different journey into the area of women's leadership and our collaboration was galvanized by opportunities to work together on delivering programmes in this field. Each of us shares our story.

Anne-Valérie

I only realized later in my career that the desire to have an impact was the driving force behind all the decisions I had made. And yet the writing had been on the wall since that moment at the age of four when I cried in front of the TV in my parents' living room, stating that the world was unfair and that I was going to change that. It's why I started working in pharmaceuticals (yes, I was naïve), why my PhD is in social innovation, why I wanted to go back and live in Asia, why I set up a social enterprise. Sometimes I think back with regret at not having taken the advice of a truly wonderful mentor of mine at IMD who had said to me: 'Anne-Valérie, you have vision, you have the passion to change the world. People listen to you. Why are you wasting your time in academia?' I didn't listen. I thought what he said to me at the age of 29 was too much (imposter syndrome), that he was seeing more potential than existed. It was the same thing with Women in Leadership as a topic. Since I wasn't a CEO, I didn't feel legitimate. I had failed to change the world significantly. So why would I talk about the topic? It took me over 10 years of being asked to talk about it to finally accept that yes, I was a leader (like it or not) and that yes, I had something useful to say. Shaheena hijacked me into talking about my career and my leadership style in class and participants actually found it useful and meaningful. And it wasn't about research, it was about what I had experienced, how I made decisions and at that point I realized the immense value of sharing my story and how this helped women make sense of their journeys.

Shaheena

My journey into women's leadership started during my PhD. Although my topic was on leadership succession in family businesses, I ended up being more intrigued by the gender dynamics in these businesses, and being part of this community was certainly a driver for my curiosity to understand more about the role of women in leadership. Fast-forward seven years and I found myself experiencing many contradictions in my career. I had become a mother to three boys, I was building a strong career as an action-based academic, establishing centres and new projects. I was the recipient of the 2006 Women of the Future award, which was overwhelming as I was recognized for my potential while struggling to be a second-time mother to a baby boy who clearly was a very determined being. On the surface it looked like I had a well-planned career. In reality, I was still the girl at school who had to work really hard and couldn't quite articulate my strengths and the value I brought to the table. I knew I was driven by a deep sense of using education to improve opportunities for others beyond my students, but I didn't know how to do this. Having taught entrepreneurship for 15 years and become an entrepreneur, I knew the value of iterating, not overthinking and having a strong dose of stubbornness (some around me call it something else!). Taking an action approach became my brand, using whatever resources I had around me to solve problems. When I experienced deep-seated institutional biases and racism in different leadership roles I held, I began to understand how damaging this is to women who have used every ounce of energy and resource to drive their leadership career. The problem-solver in me refused to accept the status quo and to identify ways to improve the situation. It's a privilege for me to work with groups of talented women, in the Middle East and across the world – every time I am inspired. The challenges women face across the world are similar; however, the creativity they demonstrate in overcoming these barriers, the resilience they have nurtured and their sisterhood are inspiring and educational. The journey for me has moved from why women, to how do we encourage more women into leadership roles. Increasingly, I have these conversations with men and women in positions to make a difference. I am certain this book creates a springboard for more productive conversations as more women move into leadership roles.

Delphine

From the rustic tranquillity of the northern French countryside to the bustling heart of London, I have learnt to adapt and thrive in different environments and always tried to remain close to my values about helping others. While starting in the legal world and investment banking, I naturally implemented what I had always done: working hard and expecting the rewards to come through. I then realized I had to decipher the codes of the businesses and the complexities of the corporate environment. As I unravelled these codes, with the support and championing of inspiring women, I realized others were in the same position I had been in and I decided to use this experience to help others navigate this maze, at work and outside work. While in investment banking I was very involved in diversity initiatives, chairing the family network, participating in diversity events, organizing informal lunches for female colleagues in my department, creating new female inter-divisional networking groups, and more generally deeply and authentically caring about others, mentoring and supporting the younger generation. Outside of work I created a circle of female professional friends who would meet for dinner to help each other – dinners would be only about career topics, with a specific topic we would have selected in advance and prepared, and we would strictly forbid any discussion outside professional paths. Advocating for diversity is not just about numbers, statistics or quotas; it's about the untapped potential, the perspectives left unexplored, and the talents overshadowed by systemic biases. My conviction is born from the stories of all these women I met throughout my professional and personal life, which reveal their struggles and triumphs amid the systemic imbalances. Today, as a coach, I provide aspiring and experienced professionals with the thinking space and the tools they need to walk through these mazes. As a teacher of ethics in finance, and a director in the higher education sector, I endeavour to connect the dots and infuse practical wisdom, so the potential of every individual finds the space to flourish.

The concept at the heart of this book, which celebrates creativity as a core competence for leadership, resonates particularly with me. Moving from a very structured approach in law and banking, I didn't believe I was particularly creative. I was very skilled at problem-solving, and solution-oriented, in a regulated context – actually relying on strong technical and pragmatic expertise. Jumping into a very different role a few weeks before Covid-19 required innovation and creativity, and it seems the vibrant hues of creativity had actually been waiting patiently within me all along! Now my team wink at each other when I start a sentence with 'Oh, I have a crazy idea, why don't we try this... ?' I particularly enjoy the sense of freedom that comes with this experience, and strongly believe in the endless capacity within each of us to reimagine, to innovate, and to craft an approach that is uniquely our own. I hope this book will help women to find joy and fulfilment in their professional journey, without compromising the essence of who they are.

Did we get lucky?

It's true to say the three of us recognize our fortune or fate in the lives we lead and the opportunity to work together. Each of us has had the immense privilege of a strong education, and supportive families and partners. Our individual sense of purpose propels us forward to challenge and improve career opportunities for women who aspire to leadership roles. We have been able to build on the resources available and develop additional strengths to create the impact that drives us. Yes, luck plays a big part, but we also acknowledge the hard work, proving ourselves to others and ourselves, over and over again. At times it feels very lonely when you are the minority voice, either because of your gender, your perspective or your compass. Having the strength to speak up and to keep going takes a great deal of grit and determination. We do not take any of this for granted. We write this book with all these lenses and have tried to ensure we keep a multidimensional approach when explaining how each of the areas affect your career. This book is written for anyone who identifies as a woman but also for men who are interested in understanding better how to support career opportunities for women in their organizations.

What does 'Take the Lead' mean?

While individual success and experience as a leader are important, how well you lead will always come down to how you encourage and empower your colleagues, peers and subordinates. It is highly unlikely that you can rely on a single leadership style to achieve the outcomes you want, depending on whether you are in a turnaround situation, a hypergrowth situation, expanding to new markets or pivoting to a different industry mix. Great leaders work with a range of approaches that they can apply in different contexts.

When deciding on the title for this book, we spent a lot of time on the title and the message we wanted to convey. The one word that didn't require a lot of debate was 'lead'. We knew we wanted to write a book on leadership for women. We knew we wanted to speak to women in leadership roles who demonstrated innovative, creative approaches to work.

Think about a time when you truly enjoyed working in a team, as either a leader or a team member. What was it about the team dynamic in the team that you particularly enjoyed? What was the role of the leader? How did they lead? How did you feel in the team? What was the outcome? Take a moment to answer these questions and then think about how you can bring these experiences into your leadership.

Beyond the clutter of research and the volumes of publications on leadership, the core is simple: you have something you want to achieve, that calls for others to work with you, believe in the same goal, and be willing to invest resources to enable this to happen. Leadership is often described as the combination of science and art, and this is perhaps the most effective way to understand the ambiguity of the term. Individuals who aspire to leadership positions recognize that this role holds power and the ability to influence. However, not everyone wants to be or should be a leader, but it's safe for us to assume that if you are reading this book then you are interested in further developing your leadership capabilities.

Leadership is distinct from management: as a leader you chart a way forward in the direction you want to move towards. Your managers have the responsibility to take your vision and implement it with their teams. Leadership is about vision; management is about execution. This is why leadership is often referred to as being a team sport. As a leader your team needs to trust you and the path you are taking. Which is why, as discussed in Chapter 2, trust is the cornerstone of leadership. Even in extreme situations, such as the famous story of when Ernest Shackleton's ship *Endurance* became stranded in the Antarctic. Through it all, his team believed in him, trusted him to bring them back home safely, and that made the difference between life and death.

In formalized hierarchical organizations, leadership roles derive their power, to a very large extent, from title, status and rank; this is power dissonance. But with speed and flexibility playing an essential role in the current business environment, companies need structures that provide accountability without rigidity, responsibility without hierarchy. The shift from vertical structures to more lateral, horizontal structures responds in part to this need and the large number of books dedicated to organizational design and architecture is a sign of their importance. International companies were designed in a very structured manner that allowed top management to control and coordinate all dimensions of the multinational corporation (MNC) – multinational, multifunctional and multi-business. If the world was experiencing unprecedented growth, as was the case until early 2000, this control-based structure was not a handicap. But as growth slowed and opportunities became few and far apart, and sources of differentiation no longer came through new markets or low-cost sources of manufacturing, companies searched for innovation, knowledge and scarce resources that were often found in locations far away from the home country.

As a result, innovation can come from anywhere in the company, and must be sourced from everywhere in the company, not just the top. This calls for greater flexibility, greater coordination and teamwork. It is about learning, exploring and working together – laterally. Today, organizations are multidimensional to respond to the need for flexibility: in other words, they need to be reconfigurable – around business units to support new product development, around countries and geographies to respond to political needs, around global accounts to serve customers better and differentiate themselves from their competitors. Multidimensional structures go beyond the traditional company boundaries to form webs of competitors, clients and suppliers.

Take the lead!

This is how it all started. We decided to write a book as we absolutely wanted to:

- bridge the gap between diversity and innovation by suggesting an entrepreneurial and practical approach to women for their careers – based on creativity
- give a voice to impressive women who have crossed our personal or professional paths so they can continue to inspire others and be role models through their stories of how they have created new solutions for themselves and those around them
- offer a positive approach to women, with fun and insightful exercises that would make them pause, think strategically and find for themselves a creative way to move forward – even if we are talking here about the smallest step
- build a canvas that could be used in academic programmes or by corporates thinking about innovative and practical aspects of diversity, equity and inclusion (DE&I), based on data and real-life testimonies.

So the adventure began, and the book features four key elements:

- The **canvas** as a place to spark creativity
- The **gallery** of leaders
- **Practical tips** about taking the lead
- **Research and insights** that bring context and depth

Our canvas: sparking your creativity

The canvas, based on a boat structure, creates a comprehensive and innovative framework for you to think about your career. We offer a practical approach, underpinned by research, and boosting your creativity around these topics, so that you can identify your next steps for each aspect. The canvas format is used in entrepreneurship studies and workshops and where the canvas is used for entrepreneurs to (define) their (business model and priorities). The idea is to create a canvas for women's careers, as they would if they were launching their businesses.

We have endeavoured to separate and assess these Seven Cs, so that luck is not the first response to how women got where they are. Attributing one's success to luck does not train the person to grow their confidence in the capacity of their own resources to move forward and be successful.

THE 7 CS – 7 SEAS
- We start with Creativity, our first C
- 2nd C is Compass
- 3rd C is Courage
- 4th C is Connections
- 5th C is Champions
- 6th C is Curating teams and
- 7th C is Career

Depending on where you are in your own career, or in your own thinking about your career, you can certainly decide to jump in directly with each of these chapters in your own preferred order. The common thread for each chapter will be the onus on creativity and innovation, as at the heart of the book is our belief that being able to find innovative solutions to problems is what makes us grow and seize opportunities, and therefore gain confidence in a virtuous circle.

The gallery of leaders

Through the stories of the women we have interviewed for this book, you will find role models and traits that you can resonate with. They live across six continents, from Canada and the US to Singapore and India, and many have lived in several countries, having grasped with different cultures, have lived exciting experiences, having doubts and achieving parts of what they wanted to achieve. They work and have worked in big corporations, or moved to entrepreneurships, changed trajectories, felt there were accidents in their careers, but stood up and learnt from each failure, immediately or with hindsight.

And in particular, faced with uncertainties, with imbalance, with unfairness, they have learnt to create and advocate for their own solutions, they have found and fought for the way they could themselves move forward, because it was working for them, for their companies, their division, for their community or for their families.

Practical tips about taking the lead

This book also features practical tips about how you can reflect on your current priorities and move forward and take the lead! In each chapter we have added three boxes entitled' Take the Lead!', which will propose exercises for you for self-reflection, and we hope this will make you pause and think about your practical next steps. Very often a slight change will impact the trajectory, and we hope these boxes will give you the opportunity to pause and think.

Research and insights

Finally, if like us you love trying to understand why, we have added research pieces to give thoughtful context and depth to the explanations.

So, whether you decide to read front to back, or dip into the book following the testimonies or the exercises, it is now time to set sail!

FIGURE 0.1   Take the Lead canvas

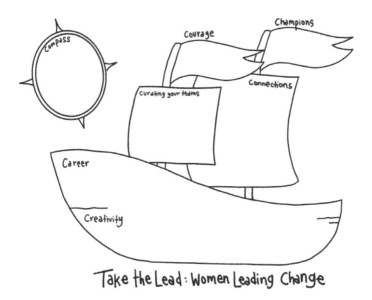

CHAPTER 1

Creativity

Introduction

We are ready to hoist our sails. To chart our course, to fill our sails with the welcome winds that will be ours. Those of courage. Of change. Of connections. Tucked below deck there is a little luck. A lot of determination and skill. A pinch of uncertainty. And a great deal of creativity.

Problem-solving. Creativity. Imagination. Innovation. Whichever word you choose, we converge on the importance of the skill. The World Economic Forum identified creativity as one of the key traits for leadership over the next decade in an environment in which continuous change is accelerating. The post-pandemic narrative labelled our time the 'new normal', but, in reality, we are only dealing with the 'next normal' – there are many more 'normals' to come. Leaders recognize they need to take different approaches to address the next wave of challenges they are facing. And there is no doubt that women play a critical role in reinforcing innovative approaches to working styles and solutions.

Yet creativity remains a daunting word for many. In this chapter, we will provide you with tools and frameworks to both dispel some of the fears you may have around creativity, and harness its power. In fact, we believe the skills so essential in today's world (one in which all else in organizations has been streamlined, rightsized, standardized – so that competition can only come from a 'think different' approach) that you will find innovation and creativity to be the red thread that runs across all chapters.

Over the course of your leadership journey, your creativity and problem-solving skills will grow. Just as a sailor harnesses the wind's power, your sails will catch the winds of challenge and uncertainty and use them mindfully and purposefully. As a sailor becomes more skilled in navigating both calm and stormy seas, likewise you build your capabilities in innovation and adaptation.

Creativity is about seeing the world differently, bringing variety and diversity into your thinking. When we run workshops on diversity and innovation, we start by asking the group how comfortable they feel about their creativity. A few individuals will throw up their hands with great confidence, others will sheepishly raise their hands in a shy manner, and the rest, the majority, will sit firmly with no hands up. The ones whose hands shoot up are usually self-proclaimed artists, performers or creative types. There is no doubt these activities are a demonstration of creativity, but there is so much more to creativity than these traditional approaches.

Creativity for leadership is about focusing on generating new ideas, creating new perspectives on problems, processes and markets. In principle, these are good ideas and the backbone of high performance, but in reality, creative and innovative approaches are difficult to implement.

Creativity doesn't develop in isolation; it's driven by curiosity. If creativity is about finding different solutions, curiosity is about challenging the status quo to create demand for new thinking.

It's the 'why' that we ask constantly as children. Curiosity allows you to consider experiences and scenarios with fresh thinking. This approach is easier when you are new to something: a new job, a new hobby, anything that requires a change to your business-as-usual mindset. In the first six months of their roles, new hires are at their most curious. After this period, their curiosity drops significantly. Why? Because individuals are under pressure to deliver to set expectations and they do not have the opportunities or the psychological safety to keep asking questions. It is also a fact that many interesting industry innovations were made by individuals outside of that industry because, simply put, they didn't know it could be done...

Cecilia Weckstrom defines her mission as inspiring and connecting people to realize their genius. In her role at the LEGO Group, she leads strategic initiatives that combine marketing experimentation at scale, digital transformation, data-driven decision-making and innovation culture. In addition to her work, she writes and produces music. When we discussed this perspective with Cecilia, she insisted on this curiosity as being central: 'If you aren't curious as an individual, there's nothing that drives you to look for new and challenging things. Curiosity has this ability to keep your mind open to things, to see connections and ask questions. If you're not curious, you're not even asking the questions that might spark the new ideas. You just take things for what they are and you don't even think it could be different. Whereas a curious person will ask, why is it like this? What made it become like that? When you start investigating and thinking, you end up fuelling a lot of ideas, essentially, because you started with "What if?" or "Why is that like that?"'

Marie Planckaert, who works at Total Energies in France, shares the drive for innovation through collaborating with R&D in her team: 'For me, innovation starts by improving a product, a process, an organization etc. by continuously observing them from a different angle, therefore possibly triggering the development of a new solution for an easy innovation. Innovation starts with incremental and continuous improvement. I am always trying to push for innovation and check if and how a problem can be solved differently. I push my team to think innovation by asking questions, or offering a new perspective to the problem, launching the conversation.'

Marina, a senior managing director in investment banking, current Head of Investors' Relations in a FTSE100, reflects on creativity and shared with us: 'For me this is about challenging status quo/questioning when you hear "We have always done things in this way." "Well, why? Let's step back, question and start from a clean sheet to solve a problem." It's the everyday small things in the job that I think perhaps matter most.'

In this chapter, we will look at different dimensions of the creativity prism, and, more specifically:

- **Creativity as a source of competitive advantage** (at the corporate and individual level)
- **Developing a creative muscle** (at both the individual and corporate level)
- **Using creativity as a leadership tool**

We will provide examples from leaders across industry, as well as individual stories, and provide tools and frameworks to help you develop your creativity and innovation DNA.

Creativity as a response to complexity

Leadership today often comes with immense complexity around decision-making. As we will see throughout this book, leaders

creativity and risk can be viewed as two sides of the same coin

must contend with wicked problems, addressing complex situations where solutions usually generate other problems. In the new world of work, be it post-Covid, post-Me Too, or other timelines one associates with, what was done before no longer guarantees success.

New ideas inherently mean uncertainty and risk. In fact, creativity and risk can be viewed as two sides of the same coin. New approaches inevitably mean challenging the status quo. We are wired to minimize risk and develop patterns to create certainty. On average, it is estimated that we make 35,000 conscious and subconscious decisions within a 24-hour period.

This is one of many entrenched habits: from the moment you wake up until the time you get to work, you have made tens of thousands of conscious and subconscious decisions. The ability to make decisions is like using a phone; over time the energy levels drain, and you need to recharge to work at full capacity. The value of habit is that we have become skilled at making decisions efficiently; this is described by Daniel Kahneman as System 1 thinking. The downside to this highly efficient way of working is the risk of acting on autopilot, using tried and tested approaches, rarely deviating from this path.

For leaders, however, this strength becomes a weakness when they need to make decisions in a climate of significant uncertainty and turbulence. Experienced leaders can become entrenched in working to their strengths and limiting new ways of thinking for decision-making. For these individuals, shifting into creative gear is not easy or comfortable. For others, once it becomes a habit it's completely natural and a source of enjoyment and creation.

Think back to a time when you were most comfortable and free to explore the world on your terms. Exploration at different points in your life takes on different meanings. Remember the last time you could launch into uncensored role-play. You may or may not remember these experiences, but you just need to look at children under the age of five in your world to see how they create stories from thin air. Notice what happens in the interaction, how ideas emerge, how others respond to the ideas and how they build on the suggestions. You can do the same with improvisation through drama or music. You will see an underlying approach where creativity flourishes – all ideas are welcome.

Even when we think we have minimal creative capacity, in reality we have the potential to extend our creative muscle, thanks to brain plasticity. Adults create new neurons; this is known as neurogenesis. This is important because these new neurons grow in the hippocampus: the stem cells that develop to support memory formation and learning. Which means you can teach an old dog new tricks! If you don't use these new neurons, they don't stick around; they die. So, learning a new way of thinking is the embodiment of 'use it or lose it' for these wonderful new neurons. What better way to nurture these neurons than to strengthen and diversify your repertoire of skills to include creative and innovative thinking?

There is an important upside to creativity in the workplace: it helps to nurture a flexible stress response. Flexible stress response is when your body generates physiological reactions in response to an external stimulus, a threat. When you are in a workplace that cultivates creativity and it is embedded in the DNA of the organization, it has benefits by promoting a flexible stress response and improving well-being. Put simply, nurturing a creative mindset has been shown to reduce stress. Research by Eric Helzer and his team found that when people have the potential to spontaneously generate alternative interpretations to problems, they actually experience a lower stress response, because they have more options and a greater sense of control over the uncertainty they are facing.

Nurturing your creative muscle

Your response to creativity in the workplace will determine how easy or difficult it is for you to nurture your creative muscles. How do you perceive creativity among leaders? Do you subconsciously gravitate to creative individuals? Do you steer clear to avoid disruption? Are you one of those individuals recognized as being celebrated for your creativity? As you consider your responses to these questions, they will determine your initial reactions to your levels of comfort to creativity.

The fact you are reading this book means you recognize the value of innovation as a leadership trait, but in reality, many people face the creativity paradox. People harbour an aversion to creativity and creators; research shows that implicit biases that manifest around creativity generate visceral negative re-actions similar to agony or, in some cases, nausea. These sub-conscious biases result in individuals rejecting creativity in their work. Creativity has long-held associations with disruptions, challenging the norm, which elicit very mixed reactions. For individuals with a strong aversion to creativity, they will reject taking on projects that demand innovation or even refuse to recruit creatives in their teams. At the other extreme, individuals who fully immerse themselves in creative opportunities relish the sense of liberation and freedom accompanied by creativity.

Cecilia Weckstrom, whom we introduced earlier and who works at LEGO, shared with us that when she recruits talent, she does not ask questions directly about creativity. Instead, she uses questions about curiosity: 'We often ask people "Tell me a time when you were curious." I think this is a huge predictor of *Tell me a time when* people's ability to adapt and learn in a job *you were curious* and always improve themselves because they might be driven by curiosity – a more intrinsic motivation. It is very difficult to work out if someone's intrinsically motivated – I have used this question as a strong predictor, trying to figure out if this means that they go and find out about stuff, not because someone told them to, but because they were thinking "I don't understand this thing. I'm going to go and investigate it," looking for a sort of intrinsic desire to understand why something is the way it is or how it could be better, and, because of that, you learn a lot. This kind of hunger and desire to constantly grow and evolve as an individual is what I am looking for, because companies are always adapting and changing, and those people are extremely helpful and valuable people to on-board to fuel that process. And if companies don't have people who are up for that, it's going to be really hard to stay ahead of the game.'

Innovation at the organizational level

Leaders need innovation embedded at the heart of the organization; however, tensions emerge as this agenda filters down the organization and it creates tension among teams who do not want to undertake the uncertainty associated with change, or do not know how to effectively implement creativity and change. Priming is a powerful tool to create psychological safety around creativity. When teams are exposed to the risks and uncertainty aligned with creativity, they demonstrate greater negative associations with the process.

For these groups, change is pushed back to minimize loss aversion. Loss aversion is associated with prospect theory, which describes how individuals react to loss. Research by Daniel Kahneman and Tversky Amos (1979) demonstrated that the pain of losing was twice as powerful as the pleasure of gaining. Individuals are more willing to take risks to avoid loss than to benefit from gains. Loss aversion influences status quo bias, which is often seen when leaders remain stuck in a pattern of inertia and do nothing to initiate changes (Samuelson and Zeckhauser, 1988). Shifting the narrative is essential, helping individuals to see the benefits and uplifts, and to feel safer in the process of change.

Both organizational culture and wider society have an impact on reactions to and acceptance of creativity and 'difference'. Where innovation and creativity are celebrated for their progress, groups are more likely to generate positive reactions to these processes. However, when creativity is not embedded in the organization, it elicits far greater negative reactions due to its correlation with disruption and uncertainty, creating a social stigma effect. This highlights the importance of establishing a culture of creativity, rather than sporadically embarking on creative endeavours.

The impact of creativity can be as large or as small as your vision. Imagine generating ideas that don't just impact your team or your organization but influence every part of the world.

Amina J Mohammed is the Deputy Secretary General of the United Nations and Chair of the UN Sustainable Development Group. She previously served as the Minister of Environment of the Federal Republic of Nigeria. In 2012, she joined the United Nations as Special Adviser to the Secretary-General Ban Ki-moon, responsible for the post-2015 development planning. Amina is the architect of the UN SDGs – United Nations Sustainable Development Goals. Recognizing the need to move beyond the Millennial Development Goals (MDGs), her approach was to look for substantial step changes to bring about change. This shifted focus to budgets and domestic resources. In 2021, the UN Conference in Sustainable Development demonstrated the attainment gap for the MDGs. Realizing that countries were not ready for the paradigm shift needed, Amina channelled an innovative way to challenge systemic barriers and catalyse change by creating opportunities for people to deliver on the goals. She turned attention to civil society and created opportunities to work with the private sector. She understood that this was a powerful force for change to begin the shift in mindsets.

Amina knew that she had to navigate through status-quo bias in the UN and recognized the difficulty and disruption to her work. However, as she stepped back, she knew establishing the SDGs would provide a way forward to improve the impact and reach of the United Nations. Only through her creativity and innovation did this happen, rather than taking the easy option of sticking to ingrained, well-established processes. The impact of SDGs has transformed the way in which the private sector and government work together to achieve targets set out by the United Nations.

In 2023, during the preview to the SDG Summit and UNGA78 High-Level Week, she said:

> All our stakeholders will be here in many different constituencies from civil society, the private sector, academia, women and the major stakeholder groups. And we will have the first of those discussions around what will the summit of the future look like – the key elements that will go into that. All of this is seeking to mobilize greater commitment, but also the resources, the ambition that we have always looked forward since 2015. And trying to keep that promise, the solidarity and the determination to respond to some of the biggest challenges that we face today. Globally, we see that 15 per cent is what we've been able to do on the targets. It's abysmal. It's a sobering fact that we will come into in the General Assembly, huge implications for everyone. We have obviously more division and we see that gender equality is hundreds of years away and displacement and instability around the world. We've got the tools, what we need to come to us with much more determination with those solutions on how we can get this done (UN, 2023).

Take, for example, the work of **Michele Oliver**, Global VP of Brand and Purpose at Mars, who led efforts to shift the portrayal of women in their advertising. With almost 30 years of experience in the consumer goods industry, Michele has developed a deep understanding of how to create and grow brands that resonate with customers and stakeholders – both consumer and corporate brands. She is also skilled at leveraging purpose as a driver of business and social value. Mars has looked to the SDGs globally to inspire their work on 'creating the world we want tomorrow by how we do business today'. As one of the world's largest privately owned businesses, employing 150,000 people in 88 different markets, with some of the world's most loved brands, the impact was potentially huge. Michele explained that they measure not just business results but also positive societal and environmental impact, and senior leaders are held to account on that. As part of this, over time Mars has extensive partnerships with NGOs including UN Women and the Unstereotype Alliance, which focuses on the representation of women and the eradication of harmful gender stereotypes in media and advertising. The result? As Michele describes, in 2022 Mars achieved gender parity in its on-screen representation adverts: 50 per cent of all characters were women, an increase of 51 per cent in five years, and all historical harmful stereotypes removed – such as women being five times more likely to be shown cooking and men 30 per cent more likely to be shown as leaders. For Michele, the work on this started with a small idea in the UK to look into representation in their advertising. She wasn't sure if this was part of her role or remit, as it had never been discussed, but she decided to be brave and follow her instinct: 'Sometimes you have those thoughts and ideas that you're not quite confident enough to say out loud; I believe those ideas are where brilliance is found – don't get me wrong, not all are brilliant, but without articulating them, you risk losing out on those that are.'

Taking the lead for Michele meant trusting the environment, bringing her values into her work and backing her instinct to share a different way of thinking. 'If you don't feel psychologically safe to say "I've just got this crazy thought" then an opportunity is lost. Diversity and creativity are siblings. I was at an event with the Chair of the British Film Industry recently, and a woman said the reason she loves film is because she *Diversity and creativity are siblings* says she spends two hours seeing the world through someone else's eyes. And it was a light-bulb moment. If those eyes are always the same eyes, western male eyes, just think of all those perspectives you're missing... Think about that in relation to creativity and innovation – we miss all those perspectives. I am a leader in a world where creativity and innovation make business succeed or fail – we simply can't afford to miss a fresh perspective.'

TAKE THE LEAD!

Remember that creativity means finding a different solution to a problem you have, whatever it is – it does not only mean creating an art masterpiece.

What is your creative superpower (remember everyone has one or the potential to develop one)? If you are struggling, ask colleagues and friends when they have seen you at your most creative – what was the impact of your creative genius? How did you bring about new ideas?

What value do you place on creativity in your work?

Who do you admire for their creativity – how does it show up in their work?

If you are at the start of this journey – what's holding you back? Be honest – is it discomfort with thinking outside your box, is it time, or aren't you interested in a current project or role?

Individuals who enjoy creating new ideas are the ones who are likely to have side hustles or passion projects that give them the platform to innovate and generate new solutions. Lauren was working as a project manager for HEC in London, organizing study trips and developing corporate relations; however, her passion lay in education and helping youth build solid foundations for their life. On the side, she would give talks to teenagers, parents and educators in France and in the UK on the impact of pornography on youth. Her side hustle has now become her full-time role as she has shifted into giving talks on broader topics around personal development, love and relationships for teens, and is currently working on a start-up project for youth growth, well-being and personal development. If you look around at your work or friendship group no doubt you will find people who are similar to Lauren, with a side hustle they are particularly passionate about, and for which they find ways to work, in a creative way, outside their day-to-day work. The examples you identify are strong reminders of the multi-dimensionality of individuals as creativity manifests itself in different ways. Your creative muscle should not be compartmentalized as one aspect of your life – often your hobbies or passion project. Instead, to allow your creativity to flourish, it needs to have different avenues and for you to develop confidence in sharing new ideas.

Does creativity have a gender lens?

Why does this question matter? In the traditional world of creativity, some aspects are more gendered than others. Whether it is performance, dance or art, gender biases still impact practice and professions. In the workplace, creativity among leaders is also impacted by gender perceptions. Research shows that when creative ideas are shared, the reactions will differ depending on whether the idea came from a man or a woman. Crazy – we think so, but let's dig deeper and understand what is at play here.

Devon Proudfoot and his team identified biases in how creativity was acknowledged based on gender. The team identified qualities such as independence and self-direction, daring and self-reliance, all of which are strongly correlated with creativity. In their research they found these qualities were more likely to be ascribed to men rather than women. In comparison, women were characterized as cooperative and supportive, both of which support collaboration and teamwork but are not recognized as the originators of new ideas.

Furthermore, when women generated similarly creative ideas as their male counterparts, the women were considered less innovative. The impact of these biases leads to creativity boosts among men based on their agency and power rather than their competences alone. Wider research shows there is no discernable difference in the quality of creative ideas based on gender. Ideas are not the problem. How individuals react to the originator makes the difference in the value placed on the ideas and this needs more careful consideration for women in leadership roles. As a leader, implementing creative solutions means understanding the barriers and identifying ways for navigation. Going back to our boat analogy, strengthening the capacity of your team is an area we will discuss in more detail in Chapter 6 – with practical ways to set you up for success.

Catalysing creativity for change

Creativity is a skill that sometimes is nurtured from a young age, sometimes emerges later in life, and is strengthened through practice and feedback loops. Creativity needs a purpose, something we discuss in more detail in Chapter 2. Change is the result of creativity and problem-solving – finding new ways to solve problems remains an abstract construct until new ideas are implemented. Creativity and innovation become the drivers for change. Some leaders see themselves as dynamic change agents whose skill set includes catalysing new ways of thinking, being and doing – as illustrated by **Whitney Gore,** who is the director of business and legal affairs for UK series at Netflix. Whitney started with Netflix in its Los Angeles office, working mainly on developing the company's business in the United Kingdom as the first lawyer dedicated to Netflix global original series developed or produced in the UK, before Netflix hired locally: 'As a leader I model the ability to ask questions and suggestions without fear. We have a phrase called "farming for dissent" which is part of the Netflix culture. It means that we actively look for contrary views to strengthen the quality of the discussion and rigour of ideas. In my team, we tend to be quite daring. We are often willing to suggest something because we are not going to be stopped by the reaction of habit. This attitude becomes self-perpetuating to encourage more creativity and fresh thinking.'

For others, creativity and innovation develop as their leadership emerges. **Jennifer Publicover,** an EVP at Royal Bank of Canada (RBC), a top global bank, shares her experiences: 'I never really saw myself as a change agent, but as I look back at my leadership roles, I can see a legacy of leading and implementing change. I have always been comfortable with the idea of evolution. I'm not talking about wholesale change or change for the sake of it, but rather a focus on constant improvement and refinement. Throughout my career I have lived in different countries, worked in different large companies and had a series of diverse roles – these experiences have made me very comfortable with change. I've found the more you stretch yourself and succeed, the more confidence you gain. Conversely, when you stretch yourself and falter, you learn a great deal too. Cumulatively, the more risks you take – whether you win or lose – the more comfortable you become with risk-taking and the more you evolve.

'We are at a point in today's world where change is happening so much faster than we ever could have imagined. If you are not changing along with your environment, you will atrophy. Driving change does require a healthy dose of creativity. I've always seen my strongest creative muscle as the ability to take existing ideas and apply them to an organization or business model which I know how to navigate. I also surround myself with other creative people who can come up with great ideas that I haven't thought of or who can help me see things differently.'

Whitney and Jennifer bring very different approaches to developing their creativity as leaders, but they share similar behaviours in terms of openness to creativity and change, strengthening the creative muscle for themselves and their teams. In terms of leadership, the key messaging is to nurture creativity and reinvention for themselves and others through consistency and repetition.

Changing your perspective

Creativity catalyses change, and change generates creativity: the two coexist perfectly. The most profound way to engender creativity is by experiencing change, welcoming it and developing a genuine sense of curiosity around the process. What kind of change are we talking about? When talking to the women we interviewed we found a common thread in the significance of change they experienced in their careers, as either they moved to new countries or switched into different sectors and careers. Both of these experiences are very common today, and both need more exploration to understand the impact they have on nurturing an agile mindset for creativity.

A physical move is often described as one of the most intense experiences and embodies changes in a lifetime. It permeates every part of your being as the experience of settling into a new environment requires getting out of your comfort zone. Even if you are moving to a country that has shared values, even language, the nuanced differences, styles of thinking, means of communication can be challenging to your modus operandi.

Whatever the reason behind the move, the transition to a new environment provides boundless opportunities to develop your ability to see the world differently.

The three of us are incredibly fortunate to have experienced international moves. For Anne-Valérie, this meant growing up as an expat child, living in Asia, Africa, the Middle East and Europe. She carried this through into adulthood, living and working around the globe with her children. To date she has moved 18 times. Delphine moved to London for work, and for love. Twenty years later, she is now British, has a family and has changed sectors, from being a lawyer and banker to working in higher education and as a coach. Shaheena made the decision to move to Qatar during the Covid pandemic, moving herself and her family from the UK to take up a new role and live new experiences. Adapting to a new environment and immersing yourself in a new culture provides you with the opportunity to consider new parameters and ways of thinking. It is virtually impossible to move to a new culture and not adapt; your creativity has a chance to develop when you actively decide what you choose to hold onto and what you decide to absorb. When you immerse yourself in a new culture, with a genuine state of curiosity, your mind opens to new ways of thinking and perspectives. The values you hold will be discussed in the Compass chapter – they are still integral to you, but perhaps the way they manifest changes and adapts to your environment. The world is far smaller when you have a stronger global perspective.

The world is far smaller when you have a stronger global perspective

Helene Bouyer worked for 17 years for luxury hospitality groups in different regions of the world – Europe, Asia, the Middle East and Africa – and then founded her own luxury and lifestyle hospitality executive search firm, specializing in the niche market, hospitality management, thanks to her extensive network of hospitality executives built over the years, working both at a corporate level or on properties, luxury or lifestyle hotels and resorts and award-winning restaurants. Helene has experienced living in seven countries; while the moves were precipitated by her husband's career, she was determined to maintain her own career with each move. 'The biggest compromise was to follow my husband. My goal was to follow but manage to find my own space. This space was my job, as working allowed me to have my own circles and environment that also gives a status, and a role within the society. After several moves and jobs, I found it frustrating to have to resign to move to another expatriation.

'When I created my company, I imagined the company being like a suitcase that I could take with me when I travelled. My business has grown from strength to strength, and this means even for my next location my "suitcase" is ready to go.'

Switching careers provides another way to nurture agile thinking and creativity. As you build up skills and knowledge in a particular role and/or sector, moving into a new area creates opportunities for you to apply your experiences to new contexts.

Michelle LeSueur is based in the US, and today leads cross-functional, global teams to provide better treatment options for haematology and ocncology patients. Michelle has changed career trajectories several times, and describes her path to us: 'I've run into a lot of colleagues who hesitated to take on a new job in a new function, such as taking on a field-based sales role, or leaving that sales role to pursue a headquarters-based marketing role, because it represents a role you're not comfortable with, or a function that is unknown to you. And I think, for me, accepting a role in a new function, which was transitioning from engineering to sales, was a game changer. After that, I was like, I can do this. I proved to myself that I could successfully navigate such a change and from that point forward I didn't have a lot of hesitation to do it all over again, because I had proved to myself that I could be successful. I didn't have much hesitation to try different things, or to change organizations or change functions, because I had learnt that I am agile enough. I also learnt I had a core set of skills that I brought with me to any role, and those were the ability to build trust, the ability to listen, the ability to navigate change, and to really understand what I was good at, and what others can bring to the table. This core set of skills applied, no matter what role I've been in. You always have to be able to listen and build trust and communicate. So, I think those skills as fundamental skills have carried me forward and enabled me to have bigger opportunities and make a broader impact.'

Other major life changes create opportunities to catalyse different approaches not only to your thinking but also to how you work. Becoming a mother is one of the greatest transitions for a career, and potentially the most challenging. Mothers returning to work experience 'maternal wall bias', a phrase coined by Professor Joan C Williams, based at the University of California, an expert in the domain of work, gender and class. Women experience maternal bias when colleagues view pregnant women and mothers as less committed and less competent to fulfil their roles, inevitably impacting career opportunities for women. A major study in 2007 demonstrated the impact of maternal wall bias using job applications to determine reactions to mothers and fathers.

All things being equal – qualifications, skills and experience – women without children were twice as likely to be called for interviews compared with mothers. Fathers did not experience the same levels of bias and in fact slightly benefited from their parental status. The situation has improved since 2007; however, there are still deep-seated attitudes around working mothers that need to be addressed. In 2018, research conducted on 50,000 individuals in 18 countries emphasized the 'motherhood myths'. The countries were spread across Europe, Asia, North America and Israel. The premise of this view is that working mothers adversely impact the family and children and reinforce the gendered norms; men earned and women managed domestic responsibilities at home. What is most striking, despite the legislation and socio-economic framework of the country, the findings were similar across countries, despite having progressive parental leave in places such as Canada and Sweden.

Mothers must contend with the biases and also navigate an infrastructure that may not always provide sufficient support for their return to work. Organizations that have a strong infrastructure to support mothers signal their commitment to attracting and retaining these employees as a valuable resource. However, many mothers returning to work experience patchy resources or nothing at all.

Gwen Billon, a senior investment banker in London, felt quite lonely when trying to navigate her return to work when she had her first child. Her hours were very extensive and unpredictable, so she needed to protect time to spend with her child and needed a creative way to achieve this. Gwen shares her experiences and how she channelled a creative approach to her new situation. 'When I came back from my first maternity leave, I was the only woman in my team in that situation and it was hard to see how I could spend time with my child. I decided to block my calendar between 6 and 8 pm every day. No one told me to do this, nor did I ask anyone if I could do it and no one challenged me. At the same time no one was going to tell me I could do this because they had never been through this before. You need to develop your own coping mechanism which suits you and your family. You must forge your own path because there is nobody you can emulate. It is exciting because you have creativity in what you are doing, but it is daunting as you are breaking new ground.'

The challenge for many mothers returning to work is allocating resources, and in particular time. **Delphine Mourot-Haxaire** shares an example of how she shifted her perspective on time spent in meetings and the impact this had on shaping her leadership: 'I remember when I immediately came back from maternity leave; I was literally fuming when people were wasting their time on phone calls agonizing about when the next call should take place! I had lost this type of patience: if I was to be away from my baby, it was to be efficient and outcome-focused and not losing one minute. After a few days, the usual pace came back naturally, but there was a shift and a readaptation necessary, related to the use of time, given how precious the time had become.'

Delphine Inesta, who is a partner in a turnaround fund in Paris, and a mum of three young children, directly links the maternity impact at work to creativity when asked about how she has innovated in her work environment: 'What is very different for the people who are working with me compared to when I was their age and working with a purely male environment is that I have this strength in me to say that my family is first and work is second and everyone knows that. Change and creativity are very much about sharing with the younger generation the fact that family matters and that it is normal and necessary to take some time for taking care of sick kids for example, and for men, to help their wives after the birth of their babies.'

Embracing creativity and innovation as a leader

Moving into practical aspects, creativity is not a solo sport: as a leader you have a pivotal role in nurturing a culture of innovation for your teams. Diversity is the baseline, but the composition of a team does not automatically generate creativity and innovation. Your role as a leader is essential to diffusing innovation across your teams to cultivate a culture that supports innovation. Successfully nurturing innovation results when key components come together. How you curate and lead your team is critical and we discuss the key elements in Chapter 6 – this links back to psychological safety, trust and vulnerability.

creativity is not a solo sport

Cecile Hillary has always made a point of hiring very diverse team members during her career in finance. Today, as the Group Treasurer at Lloyds, she has continued to follow her path: 'A team is efficient when you hire diverse people. I thought that by hiring the best people I've always ended up with stronger performance and I think that the team was clearly better in terms of its creativity. Diversity is about more than gender or ethnicity. Social mobility is also very important in terms of having different types of ideas. It is a massive promoter of change, creativity, new ideas, by having new discussions and productive culture.

This is a very self-fulfilling positive prophecy, and you consciously adapt your leadership style to the diverse teams you interact with.'

TAKE THE LEAD!

Look at your organization – where do new ideas emerge from? Is it from a leadership group or does it run across the structure?

Do new ideas emerge in response to client/market needs?

Where does innovation emerge for internal changes?

Is there a process in meetings to generate new ideas?

How often do you ask others for new ideas?

What value is placed on creativity in your work?

Do you feel you can safely share a 'crazy idea'?

Overcoming barriers to creativity

As we delve deeper into the realm of creativity, we encounter barriers that can limit our imaginative spirit. We now turn our gaze towards two of creativity's adversaries: rigidity and perfectionism. Rigidity can trap us within the confines of our comfort zones, while perfectionism, with its unrelenting demand for flawlessness, can paralyse us with the fear of failure. Yet, it is through understanding these foes that we gain the power to dismantle their influence.

Rigidity

Remember creativity carries emotional baggage. Creativity and cognitive flexibility are associated with dopamine and in particular the flow of dopamine around the cerebral cortex. This means dopamine is powerful, it is part of higher intellectual functions, and it helps us to feel good. When we are relaxed, we are more likely to be creative; when we generate new ideas, we feel good, and we feel protective of our ideas. What happens when you share an idea, and someone shuts it down without considering your perspective or valuing your thinking? Fixed mindsets are black and white with very little shades of grey and it can be incredibly demoralizing working with someone or for someone who demonstrates this behaviour. Organizations unintentionally kill creativity by prioritizing ideas that are convenient and easy to implement. As a result, managers entrench processes into their organization which restrict originality and creativity.

Have you ever heard the phrase 'curiosity killed the cat'? It's not a particularly nice phrase but, if you've heard it, the chances are it was when you were younger and a way of telling you to stop asking questions. As we know, curiosity is the bedrock of creativity, but it's far rarer than we expect. As leaders become more experienced and move into senior roles, there is an assumption that they know more, and have answers to all the questions thrown at them. Expressing uncertainty can mean losing face or weakening their position, and this can be even more challenging for women when they are in the minority in an organization.

Assuming the position of being an oracle demonstrates a lack of curiosity, with the perspective I know better and I'm not willing to listen to others, nor am I willing to learn from others. As discussed earlier, curiosity is contagious; if you as a leader demonstrate it, then others will follow you. By the same token, if you shut down curious conversations, you signal this attitude is not valued and instead reinforce rigidity and group thinking. If you have grown up in an environment where you are valued for strong performance, breaking out of this perception can be terrifying.

Nurturing agility means nurturing curiosity, and as with any learnt behaviour it takes time, consciousness and effort. At this point, developing the practice around micro-habits is important, developing phrases that allow you to nurture curiosity by asking questions that do not undermine your authority. Phrases such as 'I wonder what would happen if we...' or 'I'm curious to know if there is...' allow non-judgemental discussions to follow. Remember, as with micro-habits, consistency is the key; it will take others a while to move from rigidity to agility – provide them with curiosity and give them the space to experiment. For leaders, curiosity is a minefield; while they value the outcomes it brings, there is push-back to curiosity and creativity because it is considered difficult to handle.

Perfectionism

At this point let's turn our attention to another barrier to creativity and innovation, a perennial favourite: perfectionism. Perfectionism is a double-edged sword for women: women over-prepare to compensate for imposter syndrome (which will be tackled in Chapter 3) and we have seen from some very high-profile female leaders that this approach has served them well in their careers. Within leadership there are times when prepara-tion and striving for perfectionism are essential, but it's equally important to have the agility to switch into experimentation for problem-solving. Perfection can lead to creativity paralysis.

Perfectionism in the workplace manifests from three different perspectives: a 'self-oriented' version where the pressure to perform is internally driven; an 'other-oriented' type where colleagues hold each other to high standards; and a 'socially prescribed' version – individuals feel their progression is contin-gent on meeting the (impossible) expectations of those around them. This last group is particularly prone to stress. The fear of being ostracized for making mistakes is a stronger predictor for burnout, rather than holding yourself to higher standards. Individuals' inability to take risks is linked to avoiding failure or criticism that can adversely impact their self-image. Understanding the desire for perfection is important for you if you recognize these traits in yourself, but more importantly you may also have team members who are perfectionists.

Katherine Morgan Schafler's book *The Perfectionist's Guide to Losing Control*, aimed at women, helps to unpick some of the misperceptions around perfectionism. Perfectionists are driven by the need to feel worthy and this manifests in their endeavours and academic, sports or professional achievement. For a perfectionist, success is correlated with love and value. Schafler argues that perfectionism has been demonized by cultures that institutionalize negative behaviours and attitudes towards women, whereby 'adaptive' perfection has been sidelined by a dominant toxic approach.

Adaptive perfectionism occurs as individuals set realistic goals and allows for the prospect of failure providing a learning opportunity. However, for many women the narrative around perfection in the workplace is aligned with anxiety, aiming for unattainable standards and not being able to handle failure, thereby reinforcing an image of the fragile female worker. The extent to which you agree with this view will depend on your own experiences and how women are treated in society. The experiences will shape the narrative and when unchecked will reinforce behaviours to diminish women's ambitions.

Perfectionists are not great for team cohesion; perfectionists are considered to be less sociable relative to non-perfectionists. While perfectionists are rated as more competent than non-perfectionists, in reality people want to work with people they enjoy being with.

TAKE THE LEAD!

- Think about a time where you believed your answer/product/ performance was below par.
- What was the impact? Both in terms of real impact and perceived impact.
- How much agency did you have?
- What led you to believe you were not delivering at an acceptable level? Who decided this?

- If you can be objective, were you given (or did you sign up for) an impossible mission?
- Can you be kind to yourself and find the positive in what you achieved?
- Have you ever considered that it might be exhausting for others to be around a perfectionist? That setting impossible standards is something not everyone finds stimulating? If that is the case, what should you – or what do you want to – do about it?
- In the end, was 80 per cent actually good enough?

CREATIVITY IN RADICALLY UNEXPECTED SOLUTIONS – SARAH'S STORY

Sarah de Lagarde was run over by two London Underground trains in September 2022, with her arm and leg needing to be amputated. We met with Sarah a few months later, when an AI-operated arm had just been fitted, and were inspired by her incredible story of courage and strength – and decided to share her story in our Creativity chapter. You will see why – faced with unexpected circumstances, it is through willpower, strength, resilience and absolute focus, but also with a touch of creativity and innovation, that Sarah has been learning to continue life 'in her new skin, with 20 per cent of her missing'. In the crucible of crisis, where seconds count and uncertainty reigns, the convergence of problem-solving skills and creativity takes on an unparalleled significance. When faced with life-threatening accidents or dire circumstances, the ability to think swiftly and innovatively can mean the difference between chaos and control. Sarah's testimony delves into the pivotal role of problem-solving prowess amid the direst of odds.

'My moment of courage was sparked by one specific action – cheating death. As I fell through the gap, I remember how time slowed as I tumbled backward into the darkness. I had time to think, "Oh no, this is not where I'm meant to be. I'm in danger." I shored up all the courage I could muster and forced myself to think, "No, I'm not supposed to be here. I'm supposed to go home. I'm supposed to be with my family, daughters and husband." I needed to save myself and return home to them. However, the pull towards darkness is powerful, and part of you considers death is a good outcome. After all, it would stop the pain. But then, my overriding thoughts were about me being with my children. As the adrenaline kicked in, I flipped a switch in my brain; the pain disappeared, and my survival instinct roared. I almost heard myself think, "No, I'm not giving up. I'm not dying here. I will survive and get home to be with my family." I was acutely aware at that point that nobody heard me. Nobody saw me. Not only did I risk bleeding out, but another train could enter the station and harm me again – which happened.

'Once somebody sounded the alarm, I knew an ambulance would take a while to get to me. I had to focus on my endurance. As I was severely injured, I needed to save my energy for potentially quite some time. I told myself not to panic. I managed to slow down my heartbeat to reduce blood flow. There were lots of small decisions that contributed to not dying that night. And I think part of it comes from my job because I work in communications, mainly in change and crisis communication. My 20 years of working in this profession taught me that most people lose their cool in a crisis. Nobody likes unexpected change. We are hardwired to resist it and seek out the comfort and safety of routine. I never panic on the job, because I am expected to analyse the situation, listen to the problem, and then step in with the solution. I firmly believe that my professional experience prepared me in some way not to panic when I found myself in a crisis.

'I remember going through the usual crisis plan steps with surprising clarity. Plan A was to call for help – but nobody was around, and support didn't come. I activated Plan B to find my phone, which had fallen out of my hand onto the tracks about two metres away. I had to retrieve it – with a severed arm and leg? I don't know how I managed it, but I recovered the phone centimetres away from the live power line – risking electrocution, crawled back and then tried to open my phone with facial recognition. But because I had broken my nose and front teeth and had a cut under my chin, my face was covered in blood, and the phone didn't recognize me. I had no choice but to activate Plan C: can I open my phone by typing in the passcode using my non-dominant hand? Unfortunately, my fingers were wet. And the phone was wet, and everything else was wet. There was nowhere to wipe it dry. I remember putting my phone in my pocket and thinking, "Okay, I've exhausted all my options. We must return to plan A and call for help because my voice is still there." I did that for 15 minutes. I shouted, "My name is Sarah Lagarde, and I don't want to die. Somebody, please help me."'

As Sarah's experience shows, during such a life-altering accident every aspect of her being is transformed. Doing simple tasks that she had previously taken for granted required a whole new approach to problem-solving. Sarah's story is one of resilience and innovation, where the fusion of problem-solving acumen and unbridled creativity becomes a beacon of hope.

'The theme of creativity speaks to me, mainly because it allowed me to survive in that moment and helped me overcome everyday challenges. Still, to this day, I struggle with the smallest things. I have to think about how to put toothpaste on my toothbrush and brush my teeth with my left hand. How do I open a bottle of water with one hand? How do I open parcels? How do I pick up my cat?

'The list of challenges is extensive, and I needed to find creative workarounds all the time for almost everything. What if I had to take a shower without a wheelchair? I had a light-bulb moment and bought a silicone sleeve to protect plaster casts from getting wet. While I hadn't broken my leg, I figured a prosthetic leg would be similar. I was delighted when it worked, despite not being designed for amputees. Standing in the shower after nine months of sitting down felt like a sweet victory. It's a minor detail, but by breaking the classic thought processes and thinking across categories, I found a way to reinvent a product's purpose. And that's where the innovation happens, because I spotted some immediate design flaws for this new purpose – adding an anti-slip layer on the bottom, for example. That is where the innovation happens.

'And since the accident it happens all the time. I've read some fascinating studies on neuroplasticity. When we are children, our brains are very malleable; we absorb bucketloads of information to survive, master our environment and thrive. We learn at great speed since everything's new to us. However, at some point, neuroplasticity fades around the age of 25. And that's because we have learnt most of the things we need to live in our set environment. And we find shortcuts, so we no longer need to think about it. Take, for example, our daily journeys; we drive to work every day using the same route. We don't really think about that route anymore. We rarely need to remember how we got from A to B because it becomes a routine. My neuroplasticity was relatively low when the accident happened, and I had to relearn everything from scratch.

'I soon realized that my neuroplasticity was back, and my brain was expanding. I could retain information faster than before, like reading an article, automatically remembering all the details, and reiterating those details at a meeting later that day.

'And then I noticed that the speed at which I could read had increased. I first saw it when my husband and I would read a text together. I would be finished and ask him, "Are you still reading?" He would be halfway through. We tested it a few times and tried it with others. The result was the same each time. It's a strange but handy superpower.

'I further noticed a heightened sense of the dangers in my vicinity – for example, I would be in the passenger seat of our car, texting on my phone, but would somehow, in my peripheral vision, see the red light and shout, "Brake!" In essence, the alert system in the brain is still operating on high alert and scans for danger continuously, which also explains why I am generally more tired.

'Achieving neuroplasticity is incredibly exciting because it means that we can all rewire our brains at any point in time by doing something out of the ordinary. We change our patterns, and relearn to think differently. When you are taken out of your comfort zone, you become creative because you must build these new shortcuts to make you feel safe again, find new mechanisms and innovate.

'Diversity is vital for modern society because it prompts people to think differently. It confronts us with other ways of doing things. Over time, this should increase an individual's neuroplasticity and achieve more significant innovation – and, through those innovations, make everyone's lives easier.'

Stepping back into the realm of work after a life-altering accident is a journey imbued with transformation and adaptation. In Sarah's story, the symbiotic dance between problem-solving skills and boundless creativity takes centre stage again. While Sarah had experienced seismic shifts in her existence, her colleagues had an arm's length perspective of her experiences. While Sarah had achieved huge strides, she also had to think about how her teams adapted to her new situation.

'Returning to work was a big deal because I look physically different. My vulnerability is apparent. I have a high-powered job, being close to senior management, the executive committee, and the firm's board. I'm also a board member of the foundation of my company, and I had to go back looking disabled, being disabled, having to describe myself as disabled, and it's tough. In my absence, I had to hand over my responsibilities as team leader to my second in command. I have a team of eight, so management was a big part of my job – I'd like to add that I love my job. I spent 20 years building my career from the ground up. I started at the lowest ranks, fought for every promotion, and moved to a different company when doors would close on me, to continue my career path to the top. Four years ago, I joined an asset management firm as global head of communications. I was happy, proud and excited about the opportunity – my vision was to create a very innovative team that would act as a start-up company in a corporate structure. I wanted them to be collaborative, creative and excited to do their job. And every person I recruited fitted that bill. They are all from different backgrounds. I have an extremely diverse team, and from the outside, you wouldn't see what the common thread to all these people is because they have nothing in common. But they do: they are all excellent at their profession because of their passion for what they do. Despite their perceived differences, they have shared values; their skill sets and characters are complementary.

'It was challenging for a consumed professional like me to let go of a job I enjoy. Still, my post-injury rehabilitation took priority, and my work passion took a back seat. I returned part-time, four months after the accident. I couldn't resume my job entirely and being there but not being there was tough. But we found a way to work through this. It was not straightforward and took much trying out of new things as it was a situation that no one had experienced before at work. My HR professionals have never experienced a case like mine before. My boss didn't know, I didn't know, my team didn't. My internal clients didn't know – we needed to figure out how to navigate this new set-up. However, after months of exploring options, I aim to resume some of my responsibilities, but not all, and carve out an evolved position. I've changed, my team has changed, they have stepped up, and I am no longer the same person I was before. It would be a wasted opportunity not to innovate. This positive outcome happened because our dialogue was constant. Many negotiations fall flat because people generally are unwilling to have an open mind and take risks. Having the psychological safety to say "We'll give it a try and test it" and trust each other."

Conclusion

Every organization has an innovation and creativity priority clearly stated somewhere in the marketing material – as creativity is key to the success and sustainability of most organizations. However, implementing creativity and innovation requires leadership to have a collective growth mindset and nurture an openness for change. Curiosity drives creativity but leaders are nervous about unleashing curiosity and not being able to manage colleagues. Fear becomes the dominant emotion and arrests the development of curiosity, creativity and innovation. The next chapters about Compass and Courage will address these points.

creativity is key to the success of most organizations

Throughout every chapter in this book, we will refer to how curiosity and creativity drive progress for your leadership canvas and in developing this skill you have the potential to strengthen your leadership capabilities in creativity and innovation for yourself and your team! Going back to the boat metaphor, creativity as a sail will symbolically steer you through uncharted waters, adapting to each wave's whims, and finding novel routes when familiar horizons fade from view. Women we met strongly thought that no obstacle is insurmountable, and no adversity unbeatable. As you navigate the tides of life, these creative sails are your companions, charting a course towards unexplored shores.

Add a spark of creativity to your **canvas**:

- Try the balcony approach. Imagine standing on a balcony overlooking the sea, gentle waves rippling on the beachfront. Think about key moments representing changes, becoming a mother, caring for vulnerable family members, moving to a new country, moments that have required you to find new solutions.

- How did you go through this change process? Did you do research – if so, was it through reading, podcasts or observing others? Who were your reference points? How did you generate solutions? Did you map out as many as you could, or try each idea one by one – iterating and learning fast? How and when did you incorporate feedback and from whom? Did you enjoy the process or was it uncomfortable and a little stressful?

- Here is perhaps the most important question: did you really consider the problem before you started problem-solving? There is a tendency to assume you know the problem, without fully exploring it and being able to articulate it. If you don't spend enough time on the problem, then your solutions will misfire – a little or a lot.

- Now you understand yourself a little better, how do you keep moving this behaviour forward?

- Identify a creative buddy – someone who you admire for their creativity – and share your plans around when you aim to practise and strengthen your creative thinking. Ask for feedback and suggestions on how you strengthen your creative muscle – treat it like gym training. Find someone who does this well and learn from them until you can develop your own process and style.

CHAPTER 2

Compass

The nature of determining one's location and one's route changed with the invention of the sextant in the 18th century. Its 60 degree angle allowed for more precise measurement between the moon and nearby stars. Similarly, the compass helps us find our route on land using the magnetic north. Whatever the tool, plotting one's path is an essential dimension of our stories, on both an individual and a collective basis.

In this chapter, we look at your individual compass. What is the north star, the guiding principles behind the career and life decisions that you make? How do values, purpose and ethics influence the path you have charted (and what do these terms mean)? Values, ethics and purpose are all essential dimensions of our compass, as they guide our decisions, what we value, and how we want to behave. Knowing what drives you, where you want to go, helps you navigate these life decisions, which are, to a very large extent, informed by your values.

We will also look at how these dimensions play into the expression of your leadership and the organization. It also helps you navigate the ethical dilemmas found in the workplace. How often do you consider how your values, ethics and principles impact your decisions at work? And what happens when these clash with what is needed or demanded of you in the workplace? And more importantly, how often do you need to make trade-offs between a value you hold close to you and a business imperative? What if several values conflict and you need to chart a path and make a hard decision? How do you decide what to prioritize and where to draw the line? And finally – linking the compass to our canvas – how your compass is the necessary tool for courage and conviction, and how you learn to use it in a creative way for your own purposes.

As Steve Jobs famously said: 'You can't connect the dots looking forward; you can only connect them looking backwards. So have to trust that the dots will somehow connect in your future. You have to trust in something – your gut, destiny, life, karma, whatever. This approach has never let me down, and it has made all the difference in my life.' It is often easier to find the red thread after the events have unfolded. So, how does one set a compass, create a north star at the start of a career? How does one reset it later? And once you have connected the dots, do you like the picture? Do you need to change it? Sometimes, we believe we need to achieve goals that are contrary to what we believe we want: for example, a young woman who becomes a lawyer to please her parents, while she really wanted to be a doctor; a woman with immense professional achievements who would like to step off the ladder to care for her children, but who is told that this would be a waste of the investments made in her education and her success to date.

Ethics, values, principles, purpose... where do you begin?

Purpose

Purpose is one way of addressing the compass dimension and making it more concrete. Is your purpose to be successful financially? To be the best in your industry? To have an impact on society? To advance research? To solve one of the UN SDGs (United Nations Sustainable Development Goals)? A purpose is wider than the role you may hold in a single company, even wider than roles you may hold over time.

Think about scientists, innovators, rebels, activists and pioneers. Marie Curie and the discovery of penicillin. Victoria Woodhull, who stood in the US presidential election campaign in 1872. Or Malala Yousafzai, who was defiant in the face of being injured by the Taliban for attending school. These women, who are examples taken from thousands of pioneering and rebellious women, were often driven by a purpose much greater than themselves.

Discovering your purpose at an early stage helps you make life and career choices. It also helps you navigate when your gut tells you it feels wrong, but your head tells you to keep going (and vice versa). Anne-Valérie co-wrote the book *A Dream with a Deadline* (2007) with Jacques Horovitz in which they suggested that putting a stake in the ground and defining your road map, at both the individual and organizational level, helps navigate the currents and reach your objective. Setting a deadline for the dream helps you remain focused and, just as importantly, prioritize.

Purpose, values and ethics are often seen as interchangeable. Purpose is perhaps the word that is more universal and directly applicable to women's leadership careers. All our women participants and interviewees for this book talked about purpose and its importance in determining their leadership journeys and willingness to push themselves further for something bigger than their careers.

Cecile Hillary, a senior banker in London who is now Group Treasurer of Lloyds, made the point that having a purpose helps you have the strength and courage needed to move forward: 'There are several ways to demonstrate strength and you must put fear aside in your career. You must reach for objectives that are complex and difficult to achieve and that is exciting – a huge driver of motivation. I think great work ethics is daring to speak even if facing trouble, but I think it only works if you have the right network around you. In the long run, people will trust you as someone who can stand up and promote the company values – a characteristic that is more appreciated. We want people who can be transparent, have a set of values and follow the purpose of the company. For me, it is absolutely critical to work in an organization with the right culture, management and attitude.'

great work ethics is daring to speak even if facing trouble

Michelle LeSueur, who leads teams in the US on the next-generation cell therapy treatments for haematologic malignancies, stressed the importance of striving for something greater than herself, for having impact: 'I always needed the reaffirmation that I could do something impactful. I felt happy about succeeding in something, but it also meant it was time for something new, as I always ask myself, is the team and the place and the function better than I found it? If yes, it is time to move on and do something else. If I feel like I have had an impact, then it is time for me to do something else.'

Thoraya Ahmed Obaid is a Saudi national – she joined the UN in 1975 and was the Executive Director/Under-Secretary-General for the UN Population Fund between 2001 and 2010. Upon returning to Saudi Arabia, she was appointed among the first 30 women to the Shura Council, where she was a member between 2013 and 2016. Since then, her retirement years have been focused on mentoring young professional women. When discussing leadership and courage, and their impact on the legacy of her work, she shared with us: 'I believe that my vision of the link among leadership, courage, empathy and compassion is the hallmark of my professional career, and it epitomized my management commitment. This aspect has accompanied me through my life from my childhood at the boarding school to the halls of the United Nations, to the villages and communities whom I was honoured to know. It is what motivates me now to focus on intergenerational dialogue and mentor young women and men, when they feel free to approach me. The conversations are focused on how change comes about and the urgent need to understand both the context and the consequences of decisions made, both in the public and private spheres. All the new know-ledge and skills with which the young leaders are armed need to find their place in institutions in which an intergenerational dialogue takes place on how to fit the latest knowledge and skills in what are, often, old institutions, thus focusing on both ensuring the context is understood and the consequences are well-measured. This takes both leadership and courage to make all new transitions in our societies both up-to-date and also of historical value and immediate relevance.'

While corporations have a number of tools at their disposal to define their purpose, the reality is that purpose is always framed by ethical considerations and individual and cultural values. Purpose can lead to both positive and negative impacts, to 'good' and 'bad' if taken outside an ethical and values frame-work. I can have an impact as a dictator; I can have an impact as a pioneer on children's rights. Going back to scientists, when is a discovery or the purpose of knowledge good or bad? What is good or bad? Who defines it? Was the invention of the atomic bomb good or bad? Is generative AI a good or bad thing? How about genome sequencing? And who gets to decide?

PURPOSE IN THE WORK CONTEXT

We increasingly talk about the importance of purpose-driven leadership, and purposeful leadership is a strong element in the repertoire of women's leadership. Purposeful leadership describes the approach to leadership that goes beyond promotion or financial rewards. It describes a wider sense of duty aligned with leadership, where women invest energy and resources into changes that benefit stakeholders, colleagues and society on a wider scale.

Purposeful leadership is one way of defining a north star at the organizational level. This is particularly true of topics that sit at the frontier of society and organizations such as DE&I (diversity, equity and inclusion) or CSR (corporate social responsibility). A number of these initiatives are driven by the growing, vocal call of current and future generations for companies to do the 'right' thing. And so, we see purpose and organizational sustainability align to a much greater degree.

Why are these issues so important for your leadership? As we have discussed, courage is a big part of women's leadership and women are more likely to step up when they are acting on behalf of improving conditions for someone or something else. Challenging norms and improving the status quo become part of the leadership agenda and provide the catalyst for a fierceness that doesn't always exist when women are advocating for themselves. Fighting the good fight when aligned with values creates the thrust of energy and the results often require women to step out of expected or socialized norms, gendered or otherwise, to challenge the status quo.

conviction drives courage and brings clarity

In essence, conviction drives courage and brings clarity. It is also much easier to design the compass of your career and life when starting with convictions. **Tamara Box** is a partner at the global law firm Reed Smith. Tamara had management responsibility for overseeing the development of the firm's global strategy and operations, including its investments in new business lines, new offices and new technologies. For almost three decades, Tamara has advised the C-suite, treasury teams and general counsels of financial services clients. Dual-qualified to practise law in both the US and the UK, she has worked and lived in the US, Asia and Europe, and has advised clients all over the world. She described how purpose helps her have the courage and strength to make tough decisions: 'When we confer authority on a leader, we are asking that person to take responsibility for speaking up, standing up and stepping up. Leaders cannot shy away from tough decisions or difficult conversations; we have to be out front with action and commitment. Similarly, leaders must show strength in their convictions, but with an open and agile mind that can be changed on discovery of additional information or altered conditions. Being willing to change direction is essential in an age defined by innovation.'

Values

What is the red line you won't cross? We do not often think about our values framework, even as we make decisions based on our cultural, religious or family heritage, industry, work experience and the like.

Our values are tested on a daily basis, at home and in the workplace. Small and significant decisions test our values: removing a colleague from a project without a clear reason other than a demand from leadership; watering down performance appraisal feedback to a direct report because you don't want to hurt their feelings or deal with the fallout; retaining information that will impact a department because of the legal implications of early release.

Values are the principles that are deeply ingrained in your personality. They are the result of all the different dimensions of your upbringing. Your values are part of your moral compass, and they very rarely, if at all, change over the course of a lifetime. They form a system of beliefs that are often subconscious, and which can guide our decisions in subtle ways as well as in strong, clear voices.

The need to communicate organizational values can lead to mission and vision statements becoming a paragraph, and even bucket lists of aspirations. The inability to curate a short, tight set of values makes it more difficult for employees to embrace and align in terms of their values and behaviours. Take a moment to think about the values of your organization. Can you share the values of your organization accurately? How do these values align with your personal values? How do you reconcile where there is misalignment? Small leaps are manageable, larger ones are less tolerable over time. **Jennifer Publicover**, CEO of RBC Insurance, one of Canada's largest bank-owned insurers, shares the importance of a purpose as a necessary condition to driving change in large organizations and providing a road map for the progress made (or not): 'Organizations are not always ready for the change they need to stay competitive or relevant. There can be a lot of resistance because change is hard. Sometimes you need to be open to the idea of compromise. That might mean having an idea of where we need to go and if we get halfway there still seeing it as a win. When you operate in large, success-ful organizations, particularly big banks, it is hard to say, "We have to rip up the playbook and do things completely differ-ently." People tend to question that and argue that things are already working well.

'A transformation journey can take time, but as long as I know we're heading in the right direction as a team, I don't worry. Sometimes I do get frustrated when people dig in their heels and aren't willing to compromise. That's why having a north star or purpose is very important. Purpose driven by lead-ership and a clear narrative that outlines why you are doing things are absolutely necessary for people to succeed.'

The World Economic Forum (WEF) cites research from LinkedIn involving 10,000 professionals, in which 68 per cent of respondents consider it important to work for companies that are aligned with their values, with levels rising to 87 per cent in the United States of America and 85 per cent in Brazil.

The most important values focused on human capital development – career growth and learning and creating a culture of belonging for diverse teams. The greatest shift in values emerges across generations, with Gen Z (born 1997–2012) and Millennials (born 1981–1996) leading this charge. Despite the slowdown and threat of recessions in Europe, 90 per cent of respondents in the age bands would replace a job for better values alignment; in comparison, 70 per cent of Gen X (born 1965–1980) would make the same move. In the same age groups, Gen Zs and Millennials, 60 per cent argue that values are deal-breakers when considering job opportunities. Over time, with Gen Zs geared to become the largest demographic in the workplace by the end of the decade (2030), the attitudes of this group cannot be ignored.

What is remarkable about this data is the shift in the importance of values based on age and time in the respondent's career. For previous generations it was unheard of to discuss values and north star alignment with work. Instead, their values matured in service to the organizations that provided them with an income and job security. Over time there is a significant shift from new recruits being 'influentiable' to influential. The data above shows the strength in numbers and conviction coming into the workplace about how organizations and mature senior leaders need to be better prepared for new entrants who have a clear sense of values and what they expect from their workplace.

Ethics

Ethics are more closely associated with the workplace, and different industries and companies may put them forward as the most important different ethical subsets. They represent guidelines, or rules, that can be set by a company, or an organization. While values are individual – your decision around what is right or wrong – ethics are a company's or group's definition of what is right or wrong.

Ethics and their place in the business world have evolved over time. They emerged more evidently in the 1960s, when social issues and social responsibility drove social change. Companies investigated the environmental impact of their activities for the first time. In the 1970s, and more so in the 1980s, large-scale corporate scandals led to legislation and a call for ethical business practices. In the 1990s, this spread to the business of the company, and not only its practices, and industries such as tobacco, fast-food chains and chemical and oil companies were scrutinized. The need for ethical, sustainable, humane business became an even more pressing issue following the global financial crisis of 2008–9, during which time the scandals of the 1980s appeared child's play. The entire concept of 'too big to fail', the call-out of collusion between large entities, and the protests of movements such as Occupy Wall Street, led the call for watchdogs and reforms. Today, Millennials and Gen Z have taken to the stage to ask that organizations deliver on ESG (environmental, social and governance) and be driven by purpose.

While organizations are regulated by legal frameworks, the ethical standards and development of a code of conduct by which they abide rest with the leadership team. The culture of the company, its very DNA, will determine what employees perceive as acceptable or unacceptable behaviour.

As the leadership narrative increasingly discusses purpose as a driver and ethics as the framework for decision-making, how clearly can you articulate your purpose? What is your north star? How do your values and ethics evolve, or even change, over time? How do they reconcile or differ from those at your workplace?

TAKE THE LEAD!

Learn to identify moments to think about your compass.

How often do you have the opportunity to step back and really think about what drives you and your career?

Perhaps new beginnings, the start of a new year or moving between jobs provides an opportunity for you to reflect – but within the year when else do you consciously carve out the time to consider the direction of your work and what drives you?

How can you create the moments of reflection for yourself? The moments when you can take a step back and change perspective and go back to your values?

Ethical or values-based leadership?

Clarifying your compass does not always mean clear navigation. **Delphine Inesta**, who is an experienced partner in a turnaround fund in Paris, explains that you can still get confused: 'I lost my compass plenty of times, and I will probably lose it again! It is OK to lose your compass when you are conscious of it, because it helps working on finding a new balance. Being centred on your values and being confident enough to accept that you are not strong in all fields helps avoid wasting a lot of time.'

Both your values and the ethical blueprint of your environment provide the framework for your decision-making, determining the extent to which you believe a decision is 'right', 'wrong', 'good', 'bad'. **Cecile Hillary**, who works in banking in London, also shares the challenges on the importance of integrity: 'With respect to the factors of success, I would say being driven by specific objectives is of strategic importance because if you do not know where you are going you won't achieve it. Another factor is having integrity. Some advice that I heard was if something smells fishy, trust your instinct and act quickly. If things do not feel right in professional relationships with projects you're working on, you have got to look and do your homework. You need to figure out what is going on. Don't shy away. Don't close your eyes. Be transparent; say it the way it is.'

While moral judgement in the workplace is increasingly important and present as a discussion, particularly when companies align themselves with the UN SDGs institutional processes, culture and wider social experiences conflict with personal ethics and cloud decisions. During the pandemic and the crises of dealing with huge disruptions to every aspect of life, everyone witnessed behaviour that challenged moral boundaries. Post hoc, individuals can justify their behaviours on the basis of exogenous shocks and exceptions to the norms, but what does this mean for how society treats trust and moral judgement? Where do you compromise?

This question of the importance of compromise is close to **Delphine Inesta**'s heart: 'Compromising is about finding a balance. Compromising happens daily about the interests of a task, or the involvement you can put in your work given the constraints of your personal life. But if you go too far with compromises, you disconnect with yourself. I have been in a situation like that before and I realized that this was not who I was, and decided to leave my job, and this is where I reconnected with myself. The others whom I valued more reconnected with me. The answer to those conflictual situations is not by trying to change others. It is just by trying to change the perception you have of yourself.'

Demonstrating a strong ethical framework consistently is the cornerstone of trust, which is paramount in leadership. A recent Gallup survey in 2023, tracking leadership trust in American leadership, demonstrated employees trust the leadership of their organization. Prior to 2022, the trend had been a slow and steady increase since 2011, reaching a peak of 24 per cent in 2019. In a survey one of the authors runs on a yearly basis, from a global database of over 800 CEOs, over 50 per cent expressed the sentiment that their organizations harboured a toxic work culture (Gallup, 2023), with toxicity running from harassment to unethical decision-making. In the immediate period of the pandemic, engagement was high as leaders moved into crisis mode and worked to create psychological and physical safety to provide protection in a highly turbulent and terrifying environment. Even then, the response of different organizations was a stark demonstration of their cultures, and more specifically their cultures of trust. Some organizations provided employees with laptops, and provided a great deal of freedom relative to work hours, taking into consideration that many employees had to deal with home-schooling, ageing parents, etc. Others demanded that employees remained connected to their laptops during specific times of the day, with a lag in response time spanning from 10 minutes to 30 minutes. Micromanagement, fear of loss of control, conflicting values around family and work deliverables, around fear of illness versus performance, came into play, with different leaders reacting differently.

Values are much more comfortable as a discussion point in leadership, primarily because values provide the direction for work and life. Values also appear to be less threatening than ethics and strongly entwined. However, the degree to which individuals place greater emphasis on value or ethics will determine how values and purpose manifest in leadership styles. Today, more than at any other time, workplace practices require a greater focus on values and ethics; the diversity agenda, corporate social responsibility, alignment with the UN SDGs are powerful examples of how leaders have greater accountability around organizational actions. In a work environment where talent is scarce, the ability of an organization and leadership team to express its vision and mission in terms of purpose is critical to attracting the right talent.

'Doing the right thing' is at the heart of what I do

Karen Woodham is today the Head of Risk and Control Investment Banking in Europe for a global bank. She notes: '"Doing the right thing" – this is at the heart of what I do. What is the best outcome for my firm, the market, society? How can I influence and inspire those around me to want to do the right thing, even when no one is watching?'

This point around doing the right thing, and linking that with one's sense of values and purpose, is further developed by **Motunrayo Olaogun**. Working at Christian Dior, she likes to say that what she does is spreading good vibes and positive energy: 'My values are my sense of purpose. Everything I do today is contributing and accumulating to where I am going and desire to be. This solid vision on purpose does not represent just me. I am here for an entire society and community of kids. This is the purpose that influences everything I do and gives me strength daily.

'If I was all about me, and did not have that sense of purpose, I think I would not have made that decision. But I am much wealthier on a personal level. It really pushes me to take risks, to grow, to expand, to think big, and to not be afraid and keep on. It gives me a clearer sense of direction.

'If a project failed, I would learn from it. I take the lessons learnt, and reapply them to reconstruct whatever it is I am trying to achieve. I use the learning as fuel that propels me to achieve whatever I need to.'

Bridging the gap between organizational and individual values

The same WEF report on values emphasized the importance of alignment: 'People want to work for companies that care about the same things as they do and are not prepared to compromise on what matters most to them.' In response to the changing trends, LinkedIn notes a 154 per cent increase in entry-level jobs mentioning company values and culture to attract applicants. Job adverts that mention culture, flexibility and well-being receive nearly three times more views and twice as many applications compared to two years ago. In short, values matter more today and tomorrow than ever before.

Bridging cultural differences

Navigating across different cultures can be a minefield. Using a values-based framework to provide transparency in decision-making significantly reduces uncertainty and strengthens trust in leadership. Demonstrating values through consistent behaviour helps to navigate through cultural barriers and cross-cultural trip-ups. It can be easy to get caught up in the barriers across cultures and overcompensate stereotypes and biases. In theory the notion of values-based leadership is powerful; in practice it's more complicated and even messy. Working on values in a training programme always generates interesting conversations and discomfort where values are in direct contrast to each other. What is particularly interesting is the level of discomfort that emerges when groups must align and choose the most important values to represent the common values of the group. Compromising on which values they are willing to discard becomes highly emotive.

When **Michele Oliver** decided to embark on the diversity agenda at Mars, the starting point was a push to challenge stereotypes in advertising. The breakthrough moment came when Mars launched adverts for Maltesers that featured disabled actors during the Paralympics in London in 2012. They aired the first ever signed-only advert on UK TV, as well as two further adverts that told humorous, everyday stories of women with a disability – in a world that represented people with a disability as one of two extremes at the time – superheroes or to be pitied. The campaign was very high profile for Mars and risks were high for a major brand to break into uncharted territory. Michele shared her perspective on sponsoring this initiative: 'Up until my early forties at work, I was just focusing on working hard and doing the best job I could. I have always been my authentic self at work and worked to be a good leader, but I never thought about what my purpose at work was beyond doing a good job. But 10 years ago, I knew that I had an opportunity to bring meaning into my work – I now had the seniority and credibility to do more than just a good job for Mars. I had a chance to try and make a small difference both within Mars and beyond into the societies we serve. The Maltesers ads were the turning point of my journey to bring my passion for creating a more inclusive world into my day job. What started with some adverts in the UK is now a global programme of inclusive marketing embraced by every brand of Mars (one of the world's biggest advertisers) and working in partnership with the Unstereotype Alliance (UN women) to support other organizations to do the same. It is a movement and my proudest achievement.'

Part of the reason why women leaders were perceived to have been more effective leaders during the pandemic is the fact that they connect teams with values and purpose.

TAKE THE LEAD!

What are your values? Not an easy question! Here are a few ways to help you identify them – pick a couple of questions you'd like to answer.

When you look at society at large, what makes you upset and what do you agree with?

When you look at your team, what makes you upset and what do you agree with?

When you look at the behaviours of people you admire, what is it in their behaviour that you admire?

When you look at your family, how do you want your loved ones to behave?

How do you define right and wrong?

Compass, courage and conviction

Knowing the important role that values and ethics play in setting your compass is critical. It is what will guide what you do, and whom you do it with. It is also what gives you the courage to make the decisions that need to be made. **Jennifer Publicover** from Royal Bank of Canada (RBC) highlights the paradox faced by some women: 'Many women fall into the likeability trap. You need to make peace with the fact that not everyone will like you all the time. Still, you need to strive for people to respect you. That's why it's so important to follow your own compass. If you worry too much about likeability, you begin to lose yourself and lose sight of your purpose. That becomes problematic.'

Naadia Qadr is based in New York, and advises companies on growth strategies in fintech, enterprise tech and financial services. She has more than 20 years of tenure in technology product leadership, and specializes in digital experiences and risk analytics across many industries and domains. Naadia is passionate about creating innovative and impactful solutions that address the challenges of customers, while creating value for organizations and employees.

She supports Jennifer's view, and takes it further – particularly as it pertains to driving change: 'On courage, being critical of the status quo is a driver for me. "Just because" is not a good enough reason, especially in technology and innovation. This is not a new theory; I am just saying what others have said before me. What I should add here is that before refuting the status quo, it's incumbent on oneself to prepare, prepare, prepare. Have all the reasons ready as to why the current state is inefficient, subpar, and show how it can be done better, or ask for permission to explore. And be prepared for friction. While driving change, there will be conflict. One can deal with it through emotion or facts. It is a much more efficient process to drive through data, facts and objective viewpoints.'

Conflict and courage are inevitable in the pursuit of purpose. Having a compass helps you decide which fights are worth fighting, and which are not. Your values and ethical framework also help you determine what triggers you and your response. It is about what matters. One inspirational example could be that of **Claudia Parzani**. Passionate about inclusion and social matters, Claudia is a partner at Linklaters, a member of the advisory board of UNHCR (UN High Commissioner for Refugees) in Italy and is Chair of the Italian Stock Exchange. When asked what is the best advice she has received, Claudia told us: 'Maybe from an affectionate and long-standing client, who, in a difficult moment of my career when I was experimenting with some failures, encouraged me to go ahead, without caring about others, being confident in my abilities and my skills, my passion for my job, my ambitions and my ultimate goals! He told me the story about the crows and the eagle: the only birds hazarding to peck the eagle are the crows, but the eagle flies, flies high up, to the point where the crows are no longer able to breathe and then they leave the eagle. So he told me: "Do not fight against the crows, care about yourself, go, fly, and do not care about others!"' On success, Claudia says 'The driver is the passion and the enthusiasm for what I do. The idea that, thanks to my activities and my position, I can contribute to change things and I am able to "build bridges" between business and the not-for-profit world, with the final aim to leave a better society.' Linking her compass with creativity, when asked about how creative she has been in her career, her response is very clear: 'For me, being creative, being innovative is a lifestyle. Every morning when I wake up, I hope to do something in a different way, to bring something new in the world. In my career, I have dedicated time to listening to others with the idea of defining and designing my job and my role and to

Conflict and courage are inevitable in the pursuit of purpose

understand where I could have an impact. And in this way, I have always been innovative!'

Virginie Melin works in the art industry and reflects on her career and her compass, today, in a contemporary art gallery. She told us about how she developed her compass: 'I have realized over the years that a compass is very personal, and it is easy not to be conscious that other people might have a very different compass to yours. It is when you travel, discover other ways of working and thinking that you realize how others have different roots. I have also realized that people who do not know what their roots are can sometimes be lost – and there are times in a career when you can lose yourself and the sense of your compass.

'At some point in your career, there will be choices for you – and it is, for me, all about creating and innovating, and finding the platform that allows you to contribute, or create your own platform. I work in the art sector, and it is so important to keep the connection with art, as there is a part of humanity in art, beyond beauty. I really enjoy working both with contemporary artists and with clients, and I realize that having an impact on their lives and the notion of service is very important to me – it gives a sense of belonging as well.

'When innovating, and when working in trend-setting teams, it is about working together around a common goal, and aligning the team so their own creativity can flourish. I like talking about "co-creating" when thinking about this.

'The best way to achieve this alignment is to create a meaningful story. This applies for the company, for your teams, for yourself at work, but also for your career. In each of these contexts, what story do you tell? Why did you win and why did you lose? There is value in telling your story in your day-to-day setting. We love hearing stories, with obstacles and resolutions, with victories. The compass is linked to your story, and it goes back to your roots. The compass will make you serve the values you believe in and your sense of belonging.'

TAKE THE LEAD!

Can you identify your triggers (positive or negative)?

When were you last angry, and why? What drives your anger?

Can you identify the values or ethical framework that was violated in that context?

What did you do about it?

Conclusion

By aligning their course with the compass or the sextant, sailors established their itinerary regardless of the changing weather conditions. This allowed them to plot accurate routes, steer clear of potential hazards, and maintain the course towards their destination, ensuring safe navigation across the open sea. As we demonstrated in this chapter, a north star and a compass are necessary for any journey. And they are most effective when used with intent, when written by you, objectively and in full awareness of the values and ethical frameworks that exist within your context, and which influence the setting of your course. Armed with this awareness, you can then choose to consciously steer or steady the course you have set. This is valid both for you at the individual level and also for your teams in the workplace. People need to know what you stand for.

a north star and a compass are necessary for any journey

You have now spent some time on what is important to you, and the implications of this on your role within the organization. Remember that it is not about taking on every battle, but it is about knowing yourself and what your values are. What battles do you pick? How do you not feel guilty when you decide not to pick a battle? Our next chapter focuses on this – Courage: the battles you fight, and the ones you let go.

CHAPTER 3

Courage

Introduction

Much like a sailor summoning the courage to navigate treacherous waters, this chapter will explore how you can navigate the unpredictable currents of professional life. You will encounter challenges and uncertainties, but it is about stepping into the unknown. Through daring decisions and resilient efforts, you will courageously catch the winds of change and creativity, and become able to use these skills in all areas of your career.

Do you remember **Cecilia Weckstrom**, who we introduced in the Creativity chapter and who insisted on the paramount importance of curiosity? When we discussed courage with her, she linked curiosity to courage: 'What makes people have courage is often the strength of a conviction, and where does that come from? That could come from having a strong set of values and, of course, connections, but it could also come from the conviction that comes from having truly investigated something deeply. And being convinced that what you found out is actually different to the accepted norm and how things are right now. And people aren't being courageous just because they're stupid. They are more likely to say: "I've looked at this. It's different, it works in a different way than we thought, we've got to go and follow this, or explore this; otherwise, we're toast." That courage to stand up is essential – some say women are often much more risk-averse anyway than men. But when women have conviction and courage, it typically comes from somewhere, and it often comes from having looked into something and thinking "This just does not make sense and I will say it because if I didn't say anything, I would be going against my values."'

Courage at work is a broad and complex topic. In this chapter, we will focus on how you understand and use courage as part of your leadership. Courage means different things at various points in your life. When situations emerge that call for courage, the reaction is often a knee-jerk, instinctive one, rather than a thoughtful, reflective one. Taking time to think about situations that require courage, and how you might deploy your resources in these circumstances, will allow you to prepare for these events and may even help to mitigate burnout when handling stressful situations.

You may ask why we chose to speak about courage and conflict in the same chapter. This is because situations that require courage are often also ones which arise from conflict. And saying no is one of those situations that calls both for courage and for the ability to accept conflict. Following the global pandemic, and a greater blurring around the workday and home/family time, there has been an exponential growth in the need to lay down boundaries, prioritize tasks and ultimately say no. For many people saying no is deeply uncomfortable, and it is particularly difficult for women, irrespective of cultural context, social norms and expectations.

In this chapter, we explore some of the common elements of conflict and how to navigate around difficult situations. We explore why saying no is so difficult and present a different way to explore this area, by considering when and how you say yes. Saying yes is an essential dimension of creativity – allowing oneself to take a risk, to think differently, to find a new solution that works for you. But the ability to innovate is also about saying no, making the decision to reallocate resources from one project to another, to stop a production line for the sake of doing something different, to accept the conflict that comes with playing the maverick.

So, we will explore:

- cultivating **courage**
- demonstrating **conviction** – whether it is saying yes or no
- courage and **creativity** – going for stretch roles and challenging assumptions

Cultivating courage

When do you need to be courageous? It's often when you experience conflict, either around your compass (values) or demands on resources (time, staff, budgets): that is, whenever someone is asking you to do something you do not want to do, either because the ask goes against your value system, or because you believe that the demand is unreasonable and will undermine what you are trying to achieve. Handling conflict can be particularly difficult because it is hard to focus on the solution when you are highly attuned to the other person's emotions – this is the point that **Susanne Thorning-Lund,** a partner in the Odgers Berndtson Board Practice, supporting companies in the development of balanced, diverse and effective boards, makes: appropriate challenge remains critical, even if you are very empathetic. Susanne has over 20 years of board advisory expertise, working closely with companies on their board composition, succession planning and the appointment of chairs, independent directors and CEOs in her areas of expertise. She has gained particular expertise in the sensitive guidance of entrepreneurial and multi-generational, family-owned companies through their sustainable board succession planning. She is an active member of Odgers Berndtson's Diversity and Steering Council. Susanne reminds us: 'The ability to take a balanced, system-wide view is what will get you noticed – as well as delivering, of course. Being able to put yourself in your colleague's metaphorical shoes is not the same as unconditionally accepting or acquiescing – empathy and support are positive, but appropriate challenge is critical. After all, your experience and insights are what got you to the board level in the first place.'

This flexibility is helpful in resolving group problems, but not so easy when you need to say no. One of us in the team is the eternal optimist, and able to see fantastic opportunities when new projects emerge. This is a superpower, particularly when options are limited and you need to make the best of what you have. However, when multiple opportunities arise it gets very difficult to focus on what you want to do, rather than seeing the opportunities. It also becomes harder to say no when you have established a pattern of saying yes – more on that later in this chapter as well.

Gwen Billon is a senior investment banker who has often experienced being the only woman in a room, including in circumstances where strategic negotiations were at stake, and has learnt to say no and fight for her convictions: 'Handling conflict is not straightforward, especially when you work for an organization where everyone is focused on reaching agreements and consensus. One of the reasons why you are senior is because you have a strong point of view, and you need to make it heard. Sometimes it is not easy if you are the only woman in a room full of men. To have an argument, you can't come up with some random arguments just for the sake of being confrontational. It is important to think it through – then people around you will listen.'

Courage is a loaded word; it elicits all sorts of emotions linked to context and how we use it. **Brene Brown** states: 'Courage is a heart word.' The root of the word courage is *cor* – the Latin word for heart. In one of its earliest forms, the word courage meant 'to speak one's mind by telling all one's heart'.

Courage is a heart word

Over time this definition has changed, and today, we typically associate courage with heroic and brave deeds. However, this definition fails to recognize the inner strength and level of commitment required for us to actually speak honestly and openly about who we are and our experiences – good and bad. Speaking from our hearts is what one might think of as 'ordinary courage' and to be heroic is sometimes simply speaking one's mind.

We are aligned on this approach to understanding courage and applying it to the workplace: what do you hope from your experiences of working, your career, what happens when your expectations do not align with your reality? When discussing career progression, courage is an interesting word in how it's used in these conversations. Often, it's about the courage to step up for new roles, stand up for values, step forward for new opportunities. There's a lot of stepping up

What would you be doing if you were fearless?

and proactiveness, but we want to take courage further by encouraging you to consider the following question: what would you be doing if you were fearless?

Susan Jeffers, in her book *Feel the Fear and Do It Anyway*, states that part of our fear comes from the fact that we believe there is a right and wrong solution, a right and wrong path, and we fear making the wrong decision. She challenges us to believe that there are only right solutions and paths, albeit with different outcomes. If we can stop agonizing over the 'right' decision, then fear is taken out of the equation, and we step forward with greater courage. It's important to get out of your way and give yourself space to enjoy your achievements – time and again we see this trait far more in women.

Cecile Hillary shares her perspective on women she has worked with: 'There's often too much humility from women. Almost as if women need to apologize for the opportunities they're getting. They tend to be less certain about the range of skills and how critical it's going to be to a certain job, so they're always denying their success. It's important to have a certain amount of satisfaction with what they have achieved, but also to have the confidence to consider the next stage. That's something I found at all levels of seniority, at the beginning and at the end of a career.'

We are not talking about removing failure or eradicating risk, but if you had no fear, what would your work and your world look like? Interestingly, while courage is a heart word, an emotional word, the Latin word for fearless is *intrepidus* – this is the origin of the word intrepid, but it's also an adjective. From courage to fearlessness, we move from emotions to speaking and to doing.

Should we be talking about courage in the workplace?

Brene Brown's quote on courage emphasizes the importance of ordinary courage – when did it get so hard to speak up at work? When did it become necessary to find a specific way of describing courage to explain our ability to stand up for oneself and others at work?

Aminata Kane is the Vice President for Mobile Financial Services (Orange Money, Orange Bank Africa) for Orange in the Middle East and Africa, and she is, today, based in Senegal. When talking to Aminata about courage, her words were very strong – and in such cases courage is clearly linked to values and the compass she has decided to follow for her career.

During her tenure as CEO, Aminata found she was dealing with a very unexpected level of hardship. Working in a very sensitive industry, she needed to make difficult decisions: 'During extreme pressure, I was trying to steer a ship while maintaining a low level of stress for everyone. I did not want to share my uncertainties with anyone, as I did not want to convey stress or doubts to my team or bosses, or for my family to get too worried. So, as I was the captain of this boat, I worked hard, kept a straight face and set some boundaries. I told myself that my red line was to leave first thing if there was a point where I felt unsafe, but that I wanted to fix things before I left. After that I was going to leave on my terms. I was not going to let down everything I had worked for, especially as some people believed that women were running away when it was hard. At that time, I realized the power of my will, of my strength.'

When things feel overwhelming it can help to draw strength from a powerful persona. Let's consider the example of Kate, who used to keep a Post-it note on her PC monitor with the letters: WWFD? What would Fiona do? For Kate, Fiona was a very strong and powerful woman who was her role model and provided inspiration for power and courage. Kate was a gentle and kind individual who needed to toughen up and develop her assertiveness to survive in a deeply aggressive environment. For Kate, the WWFD mantra enabled her to get inspired by Fiona and build on her own strength. Over time Kate internalized this strength, but she was able to develop it in a way that was congruent with her traits of gentleness and kindness. What Kate and Aminata both demonstrate is that when you have internal barriers, having external role models is a *Courage and empathy also work hand in hand* powerful way to boost your confidence – similar to faking it until you become it – but you need to do it in a way that is authentic for you. Trying to squeeze yourself into someone else's persona will only take you so far, and can be exhausting for you and confusing for your colleagues. Remember the famous quote by Oscar Wilde, 'Be yourself; everyone else is already taken.' Inspiration and energy from others are powerful, but self-awareness and a strong moral compass allow us to build courage authentically and be ourselves, but with greater skill.

Courage and empathy also work hand in hand. Putting yourself into someone else's shoes and walking around in them allows you to try different approaches, and, in the process, liberates you from your own limiting assumptions. This is similar to the use of role models to help us assess what our limiting beliefs might be and how to overcome them. As you build mental agility you depersonalize yourself from the discussion and strengthen your courage muscle for your career. This can also be helpful if you think you are a victim of the tyranny of politeness and do not dare fight for your point of view because you are too polite and well-behaved, and carry with you your education about being a 'good girl'.

What does courage mean to you in the workplace? Are there gender differences? How does it manifest in leadership opportunities? **Delphine Inesta** is a partner in a turnaround fund in France. She travels all over the country to meet with companies and turns them around, which almost always includes the need to make difficult decisions, especially people decisions. Delphine says it in her own words: 'I think courage is very important as I work in a field that is quite hard. It's about turning around small companies that face difficulties. So, courage is really central. It is the courage of being able to tackle issues and to take a stance and positions that are not necessarily well-received by the community at the beginning. I have noticed that women often address issues in a more direct way. They do not embarrass themselves with too much politics.'

Rumina Velshi, President and CEO of the Canadian Nuclear Safety Commission (CNSC), has built her career on change, which is not easy in her current role managing regulation and governance in the nuclear sector. She shares her perspective: 'We are regulators and what we regulate can have catastrophic implications if not well-managed. There are certain areas where we are extremely prudent in managing risk, and others where we can do a lot more experimentation and learn and grow. There are other aspects, particularly in how we do our work, where there is just so much space for innovation. And if you were to ask around, you would hear that the CNSC is seen to be a modern regulator. We really have embraced the need for innovation, and the role of the regulator is evolving, just as with everything else in society, but particularly for regulators because they are usually seen to be an impediment to innovation. I have said, repeatedly, our job is to manage risk, to protect Canadians from risk, not from innovation, and not from advances.

'Having cross-functional and diverse teams, encouraging risk-taking, modelling those kinds of behaviours, rewarding intelligent risk-taking, and getting third-party reviewers to assess and give us feedback to validate our work is what I promote. Leaders need to be really accepting of a culture where failure is all right – because that's how we improve. In fact, where it's almost encouraged, because without it you may feel we're not going to improve. At the CNSC we drive a big part of our agenda and we're making some great progress in some very exciting places.

'We have to experiment in certain areas. How can we be more flexible, how can we be more focused on outcomes, as opposed to being more prescriptive on what we require? What are the outcomes that we want? There will always be differences of opinion, but one must create the space for people to voice their different perspectives, opinions, without fear of reprisal and having confidence that they've been listened to.'

As more women step into leadership roles in different sectors and regions, the idea of courage becomes more nuanced in how it is demonstrated in leadership. Being courageous means different things to different people at different times. Before we delve deeper into the different forms, think about the following questions.

Eleri mentions different ways of defining courage in the workplace: 'Generally, in the first half of my career, I was under the misimpression that if I kept my head down, then I was doing a good job and hitting the deliverables – I would be recognized. I realized midway through my career that it seemed not to be working like that, and that building a huge network was the key to success. In contrast, at that time, once when I did not perform well during a meeting, my manager called me into her office right after. I was thinking that this was going to ruin my mid-year review and I told her about my fear. She was shocked! Asked me if I was kidding. She told me whatever is done is done, and now it will never happen again as we move forward. This was freeing and liberating. No one is perfect every single day, and you are going to get into these awkward situations, as everybody does. One of the most interesting things I have noticed that has happened to me throughout my leadership is when you take responsibility and say "That was my fault, I made that mistake," the person across from you has been so anticipating you are going to defend yourself that they are speechless, become more collaborative, and then they start saying "Oh no, this isn't your fault – things happen."'

Lucie-Claire Vincent Ortiz, Independent Board Director and President, has broad international experience growing businesses and building brands in the consumer packaged goods industry, and has lived and worked in North America, Asia, Latin America and the Caribbean and has done business in Europe and the South Pacific. Building a great ability to combine strategic leadership with effective execution behind strong commercial and business strategies, she described her situation: 'As I grew up in my professional career, I noticed that the higher I went on the corporate ladder, the less amount of women in senior roles I could find. This became more palpable when I became the first woman appointed as general manager in the company, in charge of leading P&Ls and organizations. In every meeting, I was the only woman in the room. However, I have never thought about this. What matters to me is to focus on delivering strong results and leaving a business in a better condition than when it was received. Therefore I concentrate my time and energy on getting well-prepared for what is required, delivering results and giving my best in everything I do. I tackle my job with energy and curiosity, always striving to add value. Having said that, throughout my career journey I have had to deal with situations from which I have learnt and developed a thick skin. You don't get to become an international leader of organizations and geographies without facing challenges, advocates and detractors. Throughout your journey you will find people who are happy seeing you succeed and others who are bothered by it. That's the reality and you learn this, grow from it and become stronger over time. There is not an easy recipe or shortcut to learn this; it just comes with experience, making mistakes and learning from them, developing seniority and gravitas. One fundamental aspect to be successful in this area is to be true to yourself, follow your inner compass, defend your ideas and points of view, speak up and get your seat at the table.

'I am a curious learner, responsible and organized; this has helped me to get well-prepared for everything I need to do – a project, a meeting, a presentation. I always keep in my mind the saying "If you fail to prepare you prepare to fail," and make sure that this does not happen. Being prepared also gives me confidence about what I bring for discussion, about my contributions, and makes me more comfortable to speak up. Being prepared is my way of working, and one of the rules of my work style.

'The reason why it's important for me to be well-prepared is because I want to do a good job and throughout my career I have seen many smart women who remain quiet in meetings, without expressing their thoughts and opinions because they are not confident or are afraid. This should not happen. You overcome this by being well-prepared and informed. In meetings I share my point of view, and if I disagree, I just do, and if I make a mistake, I just learn from it and move on.

'As I talk about courage and speaking up, a couple of examples come to mind. There are instances when men drive the discussions in meetings without paying attention to what women have to say or disregard their opinions, especially when you are the only woman in the room. When this has happened to me, I speak up and reinforce what I want to share. I recover my power and keep my seat at the table.

'Another occasion where I learnt to respond is when you are in a meeting and you bring an idea, but people don't acknowledge your comment and five minutes later another person in the room says exactly the same idea as if it was their own – this is an example of how you have to defend what you bring to the table. In this case, I say something along the lines of: "Oh, I am so glad that you like the idea I just mentioned a few minutes ago, because this means that we are aligned." This is how I recover my power and make the point that it was my idea in the first place.

This is the only way you will grow and learn – by making mistakes

'If you decide to be in the corporate world and in a senior role, you must be at the table, and you have to speak up. In order to reach that level, you must be part of the conversation and the decision-making, and you have to be willing to make mistakes. This is the only way you will grow and learn – by making mistakes, learning quickly and not repeating them again – as the saying goes: "Fail fast and cheap." But the point here is that you are willing to speak up and give an opinion, which is part of that learning process.

'Courage is also linked to accepting authority and responsibility and embracing both. It requires being agile, curious and resilient and managing ambiguity. I see this reflected in my professional journey. It has been an adventure every time I live in a new country to lead a new business. I have the courage and inner strength to get up to speed quickly. When I lead an organization in a new geography I have to learn fast on the go, because I am expected to have the answers, as I am the leader in charge of that company, but the reality is that I am new in the country and do not necessarily know everything. Of course, I have experience and get well-prepared, but I do not have all the answers.

'So courage is having the confidence to express your thoughts and ideas, try new things, learn quickly, be very agile, humble, vulnerable and a good listener. And after that, trust that with the knowledge and experience I have, I will make good decisions or ask the right questions and ask for help when I don't know. All of this has been critical to my success.

'Being courageous is accepting that you do not have to have all the answers, or you do not have to solve everything by yourself. Women tend to try to solve everything without asking for help, we tend to be perfectionists. We don't have to be Wonder Woman. Asking for help is a strength, not a weakness.

'In order to succeed we also need to be surrounded by a strong team and be a team player. This means we have to build our network, connections and strong relationships. This is another area that is fundamental for success, and we need to dedicate time to properly build and foster it.'

Thoraya Ahmed Obaid was the Executive Director/Under-Secretary-General for the UN Population Fund between 2001 and 2010, and was Shura (Consultative Council) member in Saudi Arabia between 2013 and 2016. When asked about what courage means for her, and how it was linked to her values, she told us: 'I have learnt through my life what courage means from being at a boarding school from September 1951 at the age of seven years, all through my university years, to receiving my PhD in 1974, to working at the United Nations for 35 years, and retiring in 2011. Each phase of my life taught me aspects of courage that I might not have known earlier. But, to me, courage is about how one faces new situations and not only challenges, how one accepts them and thus integrates their lessons in one's mental and spiritual state of mind or rejects them as being irrelevant or not useful in enriching one's life. Challenges differ from one life stage to another. At the age of seven, courage meant facing a new institution away from my family and having the ability to adjust and eventually become one of the young leaders among the others living together at the boarding school. It eventually meant having the strength to accept being away from home and family in order to acquire knowledge that gave me dreams of what I wanted to be, but it also taught me to form many different families throughout my life in the various parts of the world in which I lived. At the professional level, courage meant often taking difficult decisions, dealing with institutional changes, but, more deeply felt, dealing with people, colleagues at work, partners of the organization and simply family, friends and colleagues. Being able to take a decision that makes one feel relevant and useful institutionally and satisfied personally is a challenge by itself. One has to convince others around you to understand the logic, the reason, the context and consequences of such decisions. This is the real human challenge of all – to be convincing to others so that they can walk the path of change together.'

TAKE THE LEAD!

How do you define courage in your professional life?

How has your approach to courage changed over time?

Ask a colleague or a friend to describe a courageous act you have undertaken. When you hear yourself being described in this way, how does it make you feel?

How aligned is this description with how you see yourself?

What do you take away from the story to build your reservoirs for courage?

Think creatively!

Think about a current situation that is uncomfortable and requires you to have the courage to challenge the discussion and the outcomes. In this situation, the discussion involves a number of strong personalities around the table.

Think of someone you know, who never seems to be shy, is overconfident, someone who effuses power and self-assurance.

- What would they do in your situation?
- How would they react?
- How would they get to the outcome you want to achieve?

What can you apply to your situation?

At what point can you embody this approach? What would you need to do to make it congruent with your personality?

Demonstrating conviction

Let's now delve into the power of two simple yet profound words: yes and no. The ability to confidently say yes when opportunity arises and to assertively say no when necessary is intertwined with courage and conviction. So let's set sail into the uncharted waters of making choices that align with your true aspirations and convictions, and demonstrate courage and conviction.

Saying yes

Women have a problem saying no in the workplace, but even when women do say no, they can still experience negative consequences. It's a classic double bind: you are penalized if you do and penalized if you don't. **Katharine O'Brien** at Rice University examined what happens when women say no professionally; her starting point demonstrated that women say no far less often than men in the workplace.

Nadia Verjee is the Executive Director, Global Initiative of Expo City Dubai, Expo Dubai Group, and is based in Dubai. She reflects on this double bind: 'I rarely have said no to my boss. I think that's because I say yes, and I deliver that. That's been good for me. Have I done it? Have I done it at times at my own expense? Yes, I have. Have I done it in circumstances where it has eaten into my life considerably? Yes – is it because we have massive deliverables to deliver, and we have to get on with it? Now that the mega event is over, and I can say, "Let's think about this." I have no problem whatsoever saying, "Let's think about it." Let's look at the option we have in hand. And let's look at this new option and see what's the better option. I was having a conversation today with a colleague who had a difficult discussion with another colleague – he did not understand what she is doing or why she is doing it. And I said to her, "The simplest way is to spend five minutes presenting upfront: this is the option I have in hand. What is the alternative? We will do it this way, or we'll do it this way." And just being very clear about the value that you have – and be aware of your own organization, keeping aligned with the best use of your time and resources.'

In the workplace, saying yes more often means more work, more projects, more deadlines. This inevitably causes immense difficulties for the women in those situations who are faced with trying to juggle multiple tasks. As a result, to avoid compromising the quality of work delivered, they work overtime, increasing the risk of burnout. Then why is it still so much easier to say yes to a new project or responsibility, even when you are already overloaded? Or worse still, saying yes to something that is a distraction, or something you really don't want to take on. The positive consequences of saying no far outweigh the damage of adding yet another line to your to-do list.

When was the last time you said no to a colleague, and stood your ground? Not the half-hearted no that backs you into a corner and leads to your giving in, but a power pose: the strong, hands on hips, assertive no from deep inside you. What was the ask? What did you consider? Why did you say no? What happened afterwards? What happens after the no is the sticking point; how many times have you said yes to something you don't want to work on for fear of diminishing your likeability at work? When did you first start saying yes to please people around you – maybe family, teachers or friends? The socialized and learning experiences of women often emphasize the need for social affirmation; this is true whether you are brought up in an individualistic or collectivist society. The amplification may be different to reflect the cultural norms, but there are very few instances where females are not socialized to be carers, keepers of the kin.

The desire to remain polite and therefore liked overrides the desire to assert oneself. 'The tyranny of politeness limits your career prospects', a *Forbes* article written by Shaheena, identified that 20 per cent of people had experienced being bullied at work (data from the ILO global survey). Of employed people, 23 per cent had experienced physical, psychological or sexual harassment (data from the ILO, Lloyds Register Foundation LRF and Gallup). 'The research from the ILO demonstrated that three out of five victims had multiple experiences of violence and harassment at work. The most common reasons for non-disclosure for all victims were being seen as timewasters and fearing their reputations would be damaged. While a magic wand doesn't exist, you can take a stand against the tyranny of politeness, knowing your boundaries and what you will not accept for yourself and your colleagues. Having a clear set of values valid and relevant to your working life makes it far easier to assert yourself when a line has been crossed. Once you set the boundaries, you ensure they are respected, and this allows you to steer your career. Being polite does not mean being a pushover.'

Failing to comply with norms and expectations does create a backlash for women, and saying no in the workplace does have consequences. Returning to **Katharine O'Brien**'s research, there was a difference in reactions from supervisors when a man said no compared to a female counterpart. Men did not receive penalties for pushing back; it was expected. Women on the other hand were rewarded for compliance through promotions – up to a point. As long as they said yes and played ball, they were safe and promoted, but over the longer term these behaviours did not lead to promotions to the C-suite. Women found they were stuck, frustrated and still carrying the bulk of responsibilities described as gendered and not valued for promotions.

Tamara Box, partner at the global law firm Reed Smith in London, was very clear about courage: 'It is always easier to get forgiveness than permission; this is my favourite phrase because it justifies stepping up, taking action and getting on with things. I'm willing to take risks for those things I believe in, and I advise other women to do the same.

'No one would ever suggest I am a conflict avoider, and when I disagree with something, I am definitely open about my opinions. However, I work hard to get people to agree, to compromise, to reach a win–win scenario; I call that "getting to yes". And yes has been a byword for my entire career; if I can do it, I will do it.'

Dominique, who had various roles in banking in London in US banks and is now a senior woman in management in London, explained her own journey to us: 'You should seek to be fair but you cannot please everyone. For example, in a challenging negotiation, or with your (larger) team, the audience is invariably split the same way: 10 per cent of people are your unconditional fans and 10 per cent might unconditionally disagree with you. Those 20 per cent are therefore outside of your control. You can't do anything about it. Focus on the 80 per cent undecided in your audience. Then call on your 10 per cent unconditional fans in a tough situation, when you really need support. However, do not waste a second on any group that unconditionally disagrees with you, because by definition it is wasted energy, and, in fact, if you agitate them, you annoy them – you are working against your goals. All your energy needs to be in swinging the 80 per cent undecided. Avoid seeing praise as your reward. Great if it comes, but deep down, keep your eyes on the prize, whatever it is – a deal, a stretch assignment, pay or promotion. Do not be distracted by compliments.'

Over the last decade, a great deal has changed in the work-place, with a greater awareness around why and how women say no; but without a doubt, in every leadership programme or seminar, there is a moment when this point emerges. From a multicultural context there are some regions where the macro-culture has an acceptance of no as a point of assertiveness and clarity. In other regions, that simple word is rarely uttered as it represents a loss of face and can be insulting, particularly to a supervisor. The situation is further compounded when age is venerated as part of societal culture and line managers or bosses are usually older. When you layer on sectoral and organizational cultures, as well as generational differences, navigating around no, it becomes such a minefield that it's far easier to ignore this issue and not take a position.

Don't be afraid to say no – saying no does not mean the end of your career

The no factor presents challenges as it reinforces subcon-scious biases or stereotypes that an assertive woman is difficult to work with. **Catherine Clark** is a communications entrepre-neur and runs her own communications business, which she started after a long time working in television in Canada. She is also the co-founder and co-host of Honest Talk, an online plat-form for women which inspires connections, community and confidence, featuring a podcast which highlights remarkable women who are changing the way that we look at professional life. She told us: 'One of the things that I do tell women is: "Don't be afraid to say no – saying no does not mean the end of your career. It means that you are establishing some kind of guideline for what works for you at that time." This is because we may be saying no for any variety of reasons. We may be saying no because we're just too busy and we literally can't do it anymore. We may be saying no because we have small children who need our attention and it's just not the opportune time for us, and all those reasons are valid. And what we must do is get over the fear of no being a career ender. And so, I have learnt over time that no is a very personal word. And you are the only person who can judge when you use it, when you say no, because your circumstances are different from others'.'

The enduring influence of cultural norms on gender roles continues to impact men's responses to women's assertiveness. **Sheikha Alanoud Al Thani,** Deputy Chief Executive Officer at Qatar Financial Centre (QFC) Authority and a World Economic Forum Young Global Leader, highlights the importance of asserting oneself professionally. She emphasizes the need to address misconceptions about assertiveness, stating that expressing opinions is a vital aspect of her role, irrespective of gender, fostering mutual respect over time.

Rather than focusing on how to say no, when in some cases it's practically impossible, let's turn this argument around and discuss when and how to say yes. It's important, however, to remember to say yes only when you actually mean it – the moment the brain hears a yes, it's a green light.

Research shows a no response provokes slower response times and generates a negative signal. When we spoke to **Kitty Chisholm,** one of the authors of *Neuroscience for Leadership*, she explained why this emerges: 'When you are asked a question, it is often structured so that it is priming for a positive response, so when the response is negative it takes longer to respond because it takes longer to process the response. A negative response, when there is an expectation of a positive one (for example, because you are junior, or simply female, as in the example above), is an error message, which means an adjustment needs to be made to your beliefs, and, depending on the person and the context, this can trigger emotions such as anger or anxiety. These emotions need to be managed via the prefrontal cortex (PFC) based on your capacity for emotional regulation.'

Becoming selective in saying yes means you are creating space to grab the exciting opportunity that ticks all your boxes and is something you are genuinely interested in working on. Of course, this discussion takes you to the Compass chapter: knowing what drives you will help to determine very quickly whether that opportunity is aligned with your goals or an interesting shiny distraction. Remember that not every opportunity is one you should take, not every opportunity is the right one, and some opportunities are actually a distraction or derailment.

This also links to creativity, as you need to take an innovative approach to determine the best way of presenting your thoughts. Some circumstances may call for a simple yes or no, while others require creative thinking – perhaps there are unconsidered opportunities or approaches which work better for everyone rather than a straightforward agreement or disagreement.

Creative solutions provide alternative paths for your career and one of the most striking aspects of **Tamara Box**'s career is her ability to be innovative. In Chapter 7 we will discuss the increasing trend to craft your career. Tamara shares how shaping her career strengthens her courage to assert herself in other aspects of her work: 'I've been adventurous in my career choices; I'm known as a start-up junkie. I like being at the beginning of something, able to shape the strategy and the future of a new venture, a new market, a new industry. Where some seek the security of settled decisions, I thrive on taking a risk, building something from the ground up. While some courage is needed, there's always something new to learn from each step into the unknown. That's the exciting part.'

TAKE THE LEAD!

Saying yes, saying no, and stretch roles.

How do you say yes in a way that works for you?

When you say yes, what are the conditions that are within your control? What do you need from others?

When saying no, apologies are not needed, but clarity is essential. Remember, the no needs to be heard and will generate a more negative reaction, so be clear on why you are saying no – and be sure your reasons are supported.

Practice with trusted colleagues or friends. Saying no or pushing back to someone can be more challenging than doing it in your head. Focus on the content, but also your tone, your face and body language. Adopting a neutral face is important, as a frown or worried face will heighten negative reactions, and a smile will send mixed signals.

Courage and creativity: going for the stretch roles and challenging the assumptions

Linking courage and creativity, it is all about recognizing the importance of being stretched in your career – called stretch roles – and gaining confidence through your growth.

Stretch roles

A stretch role is an opportunity, either in your current role or with another department or organization, in which you are given a role or project that takes you out of your comfort zone. It may be a new project requiring you to reskill or apply your existing skills in a completely different environment. It may be a role that calls for a leadership position you have not previously held, managing larger teams, entire divisions or leading a transformation.

People react differently to challenging new positions: fear, hope, excitement, self-doubt all come into play, even when you know you are ready, capable and willing. Some of this reaction is a function of your risk propensity, of your assessment of the pros and cons of the new role, and your stage of life.

What is interesting is the impact on your brain, and therefore your ability to rewire, recreate and reinvent, when you take yourself out of your comfort zone. You are encouraging your brain to stretch, make new connections, fire up and rewire itself as you embark on a new and challenging opportunity.

The demand on our brain to make and build new neural pathways is immense, and the learning sticks when you have enough time and energy to invest in this growth opportunity. Saying yes to stretch roles is pivotal for your career development for many reasons. First, it clearly signals that you are looking for growth. When you take on a stretch role you demonstrate your comfort and competence in your current role, as you can work at speed and not have to overthink your decisions. Consider how often you enjoy your work because it brings a sense of comfort and expected enjoyment. Some might ask this question more harshly, as how often do you switch into autopilot mode? When do you get excited about trying out something new or taking a different approach to working patterns? Does the idea of embarking on a new project, with skills you are yet to develop, generate excitement or do you worry about not being able to handle the challenge?

Growth only happens when you step out of your comfort zone

Stretch roles are important to build your confidence in your ability to handle new challenges, and to let you determine how you take on new roles.

The fear of failure can be quite overwhelming, to the point where you may feel paralysed to move forward. Failing means different things to everyone, whether it's a sense of personal failure and not living up to the internal standards you have for yourself, or whether it is because you see yourself as paving the way for others, and in particular women, or because the work you are doing is so deeply embedded in your sense of purpose, and each of these factors does not allow you to fail. While the pressure not to fail is immense, one of the strongest themes in this book is about creating space for failure, for yourself and your teams.

Cecile Hillary, who is now Group Treasurer at Lloyds, shares how she has handled stretch roles in the past: 'I think there are several ways you can demonstrate strength and, ultimately, you need to put the fear aside in your own career and just reach for opportunities. If it's too comfortable and you understand everything, then you are not stretched enough. You need to have objectives that feel like they're going to be complex and difficult to achieve. I think that's exciting and a huge driver of motivation. So that's the first part of courage.'

Stretch roles do not need to be huge leaps and are not absolute; they may start with small steps, small changes to build your confidence. The small steps also signal to colleagues that you are not maintaining your status quo, you are changing in line with your aspirations. The reactions may be mixed and in some cases a push-back against what is perceived as inauthentic behaviour from you, but we return to the earlier point: if you don't change and you remain in your zone, you aren't growing. Andy Molinski has researched how people from quite different walks of life step outside their comfort zone, identifying the barriers to change. He explains the power of customization, small changes like personalizing your coffee, and nudges to help instigate changes.

Dominique moved from a production role to a management role. She explains: 'Changing jobs was one of the biggest risks I took in my career at that time. I felt like I left strong client relationships behind, and I was unsure about it. Nevertheless, the way I thought about it gave me courage and resilience. If you are in a new role, you learn. So, I have learnt that you need to take risks. Looking back, I should have taken many more such risks, but it was just me being too comfortable and having fears. Courage is "thinking big". I have seen people grow so much, so you should set a target very high, but then give yourself the means to succeed.'

Marie Planckaert also shared her views on failure – she works in the oil industry and today is a VP for Exploration Carbon Storage at TotalEnergies: 'Failure is a very strong term for me. Failure for me is a complete screw-up of something, a bit of a catastrophic event. Therefore, I rarely consider a failure as a failure; it is just a setback that offers a new opportunity, to try something else or embrace a new path. But my view of what the term failure means might be too big compared to what it really means. In general terms, depending on one's mindset, an unexpected unpleasant event in a project could be seen as a failure by some or as a minor setback by others. More often than not, I would rather point out there is something we have not understood properly and this event provides us with the opportunity to work on the specific element and become better. I have changed countries, positions, and been seconded to other companies numerous times, and when you change positions, you must put yourself in an open-growth mindset and practise humility, because you cannot land somewhere and consider you know everything. Having an open mindset and humility is linked to a scientist's mindset, and those are the first ingredients to cook innovation. I have the chance to be a geologist and reservoir engineer by background; in my job, we work with risks and uncertainties every day, which in return build this humility and openness to unexpected events and prepare for innovation.'

Whitney Gore, who works at Netflix, adds: 'Sometimes you might make a decision that does not land well, but you should not be blamed or looked down on for taking an informed risk, after gathering the right information and including the right individuals in the conversation. As a leader, you exercise your best judgement, you learn from your failures, and you take that learning to move on to the next thing.'

For **Lamice Hourani**, the stretch was leaving well-known corporations, to trust herself in smaller structures, and gain the autonomy and flexibility she was looking for: 'I spent the first 15 years of my career in a traditional setting, working for huge, well-known corporations. Then I decided to take a risk and move to smaller companies where I would become a bigger fish in a smaller pond. This freed me from the idea that I needed a big name behind me to be successful. I started honing my own skills and offering clients my capabilities instead of the bank's capabilities. It allowed me to create more freedom and a sustainable book of business. These were now my clients and not the bank's clients anymore. I would be able to service them from anywhere. I was yearning for freedom to service my clients the way I intended, without the pressures of a big employer who invariably pressures you to sell certain products above others. I also needed to have autonomy in setting up and operating my own business, leading a team and having flexibility in my schedule to accommodate my other priorities.'

These stretch role opportunities, often outside your comfort zone, will expand your transferable skills and make you adapt to unfamiliar challenges. By stepping up to these challenges, you will build confidence, and demonstrate your potential. However, being able to identify, accept and thrive in these roles is as important as recognizing the barriers that could prevent you from seizing the opportunities, such as the imposter syndrome and the glass cliff.

Imposter syndrome

The term imposter syndrome came into the public eye in the 1970s, although we know this emotional state has been observed for a much longer period. Imposter syndrome is a lingering sense that, even after you have experienced a significant achievement that you worked hard for, you feel like a fraud and not worthy of praise and accolades. While men and women alike suffer from it, women appear to be more impacted. Jessica Bennett, author of *Feminist Fight Club*, a book that focuses on imposter syndrome and her own experiences, defines it as 'that crippling sense of self-doubt that women often feel in the face of challenge'. In fact, she notes experiencing it even as she wrote the book on the same topic. The irony is not lost on us, nor on the number of women we speak to about imposter syndrome in every leadership programme we deliver.

The narrative around imposter syndrome gained momentum with the vulnerability and personal insights offered by powerful women such as former German Chancellor Angela Merkel, Christine Lagarde, President of the European Central Bank, and Former First Lady of the United States of America Michelle Obama. **Michelle Obama** acknowledged that that little voice stays with her: 'I still have a little [bit of] imposter syndrome, it never goes away, that you're actually listening to me.' Her vulnerability creates a stronger human connection, particularly as a role model to girls from diverse ethnic backgrounds, but it is important to recognize practical ways to deal with the challenges that surface from imposter syndrome. **Christine Lagarde** described her approach to dealing with imposter syndrome by over-preparation for her work: 'When we work on a particular matter, we will work the file inside, outside, sideways, backwards, historically, genetically and geographically. We want to be completely on top of everything, and we want to understand it all, we don't want to be fooled by somebody else.' Before we start the self-criticism about experiencing imposter syndrome, it is important to note that it is far more common among high achievers and creative people, particularly among individuals who are breaking barriers.

Imposter syndrome is relatively normalized as an experience, but today it has become a condition that is self-limiting. It seems shared in a way that is almost a call to join the imposter syndrome club and share experiences of feeling inadequacy rather than celebrating achievements. How do you help Michelle Obama get rid of that little, but persistent, voice that expresses surprise when others listen, rather than having an expectation that she will be listened to with awe and respect for her insights?

Fundamentally, addressing imposter syndrome comes down to how you build your confidence, challenge your capabilities and grow. Growth only happens when you step out of your comfort zone, and then take an opportunity that allows you to build confidence in your abilities. This is described by the psychologist Albert Bandura as self-efficacy. Self-efficacy refers to how you are able to implement behaviours for specific outcomes and refers to your ability to exert control over your motivation, behaviour and wider environment. How you see your capabilities is closely tied to imposter syndrome, but like a circle made from elastic, as you stretch successfully, the area you cover also expands, addressing new skills and behaviours. This is the learning zone, which stretches you out of your comfort zone but does not take behaviours into the stress zone.

Self-efficacy is quite literally the antidote to imposter syndrome for women. Self-efficacy is a more nuanced way of addressing confidence, and taking this approach brings a fresh perspective to understanding how aspirations and ambitions are expressed by women and men at work. Research by Rosanne Hartman and Emily Barber argues that self-efficacy and work engagement are evenly distributed between men and women. Men, however, have significantly higher career aspirations compared with women. There are wider reasons for this outcome – for example, whether women have the same opportunities as men for stretch roles, whether women have the same types of role models who shape aspirations. What is interesting is that although men and women are largely similar in their self-efficacy, there is a discrepancy in how this manifests. Their research found that while women may believe they have the competences to accomplish challenging tasks, it does not necessarily mean that they follow through with their actions. To create a belief in their capabilities, self-efficacy is a strong foundation, but additional interventions are needed: championing, mentoring, coaching and training to build the self-confidence to go for those roles. The same research reinforced how women and men conquer their competences dealing with promotions – men will actively seek out promotion prospects even when they do not have the requisite skills or knowledge to carry out the role. In contrast, women will ensure they can deliver for the next role before applying for promotion.

The area of self-efficacy and gender is gathering interest across the globe, and demonstrates the importance and potential impact of self-efficacy in countries with strongly gendered norms and where the gender gap is sizeable. In India, for example, research shows that a strong correlation exists between self-efficacy and workplace well-being, which indicates that having a strong sense of your capabilities helps to address ongoing concerns around stress and burnout (Singh et al, 2019). Research on women in Saudi Arabia demonstrated that high self-esteem and high self-efficacy are important predictors of women's empowerment (Al-Qahtani et al, 2021). For these women, it is not just about believing they can push themselves, but demonstrating they have done this, to themselves and to the wider society, that has a direct impact on their self-esteem, creating a virtuous cycle for women at work. There is also a difference between typical corporate career and entrepreneurial paths. Resilience plays a role, and so does stretch.

Dominique, who has been working in finance for more than 20 years in numerous roles, mentioned: 'People do not have time to think and are not aware that they are creating (gender) bias. Less experienced managers do not leave any room for people to make mistakes. In practice, no job is going to come back perfect. There is research in finance demonstrating there is different treatment of mistakes for women and minorities than for men. The way you treat success is sort of the same for everybody, but when a woman makes a mistake, she has a lot less of a safety net around her to digest it and learn from it, and eventually make it a positive experience. She is more likely to face it alone. This mainly comes from a lack of informal network. This has an impact on risk-averseness.'

Marie Planckaert reminded us of the importance of the journey: 'I feel successful when we manage a situation such as a team, more than just myself. And success should not be celebrated at the "end" because it can be unidentified or too far in the future, so success needs to be recognized along the journey. I never worked towards having a successful career and actually you can wonder what a successful career really is. It was always more about the journey and appreciating it is important in your career, because, as Simon Sinek, author and inspirational speaker on business leadership. rightfully points out, we are playing an infinite game.'

Caroline Flanagan is an author and a coach – she was a city lawyer, who now works to increase the number of women and people of colour in leadership. Caroline's mission is to empower minority individuals to defy the odds, triumph over adversity and win battles you think you cannot win. She is a recognized expert on imposter syndrome, so we asked her how to tackle imposter syndrome, and Caroline told us: 'Don't tackle it, make it your strength. Build a relationship with it where it becomes the thing that empowers you rather than limits you. The biggest mistake I see people making with imposter syndrome is resisting it – either by searching for the magic trick that will make it disappear; arguing against it with statements like "I'm not a fraud! I deserve to be here!" (which may be factually true, but they don't believe in this at an emotional level); or by deflecting it by saying it is someone else's problem to fix. None of this works. You're still left with the same feeling that you're not enough and you're going to be found out. A better approach is first, to accept it, second, to solve how it's holding you back on a behavioural level (if you're an overthinker, for example, solve for it by being more present), and third, to make it your strength by knowing your story (i.e. why you have imposter syndrome) and choosing what you want to make it mean about you in a way that empowers you. This approach has been life changing for me, instrumental in my clients' success and is the solution I illustrate in my book on imposter syndrome in people of colour, *Be The First*.'

Glass cliff

Take a moment to step back and consider the following scenario. For some time, you have been restless in your role, and you are looking for a new opportunity, and you have signalled your desire for something new to stakeholders. The moment arrives when you are offered that coveted leadership position, but your reaction is not an overwhelming sense of euphoria. The position you are offered is not the big leadership vision, blue sky thinking, you had envisaged; in fact, it's very different. The role is riddled with tripwires, the path ahead is a mess and there are too many people working against the role you have been offered. Your job is a clean- up job, of unprecedented magnitude, a transformation. And as such, the likelihood of failure is high, meaning that the stakes are very high for your leadership trajectory. This is the glass cliff.

Susanne Bruckmuller and Nyla Branscombe's article in *Harvard Business Review* argued that women were more likely to break the glass ceiling and achieve coveted leadership roles when an organization is in crisis mode. We just need to look at recent events to see how the glass cliff still pervades for women taking on leadership roles. **Linda Yaccarino,** in 2023, was appointed as the new CEO of X (previously known as Twitter), taking over from Elon Musk and having the herculean task of trying to salvage a company in total crisis.

The logical approach would be to run from the glass cliff, to avoid accepting a high stakes/high failure assignment, but there is a different side to consider. In areas where career paths are still blocked for marginalized groups – be they women or ethnic minorities – high-risk promotions and glass cliff appointments are more likely to be offered to these groups than to white men. This practice is particularly true for women in countries with higher levels of gender inequality (Morgenroth et al, 2020). This risk tax, described by Glass and Cook (2020), requires minority groups to prove themselves to be worthy of senior leadership positions. When a woman is appointed to a glass cliff leadership position the stakes are higher, particularly when they are in the minority holding leadership positions. The chances of failure are high and if they fail the negative fallout is not limited to that individual, but the risk is that they are seen to represent the inadequacies of their group. Is this reasonable? Of course not, but it is the enormous burden women in these roles carry and the same is true for ethnic minorities.

The unstable, uncertain, complex and complicated world of today requires that leaders demonstrate the ability to navigate through difficult situations, so if we turn this thinking on its head, then the glass cliff provides an opportunity to develop self-efficacy in its most extreme form and strengthen leadership resilience and adaptability to build crisis leadership skills applicable to different sectors.

Jennifer Publicover, in the financial industry in Canada, says: 'Many senior leaders suffer from imposter syndrome and don't always have a strong belief in themselves. But I find that the more I advance in my career, the more I believe in myself and my purpose. I attribute that to the strong leaders I have around me – they really support me, give me opportunities and believe that I can make change happen. That makes a huge difference.

'Today, I have the confidence to speak up. I have the courage to push myself and stand up in front of a CEO or a board of directors to sell my vision. From a young age, I believed in doing the right thing and, as I moved up in my career, I became more convinced of my voice and speaking up. I went from trying to do the right thing for people, to also trying to do the right thing for the business or organization.

'Jonas Valančiūnas, the basketball player, says it well – you do not get better without failure. Not everything is going to work out the way you think, but you must learn from it. Everything is a learning experience and I do not get too worked up if things go wrong. Testing and learning are all part of evolving. You need to focus on making the most informed decisions and have confidence that things will go the way you want, but ultimately, accept that not everything will go perfectly right.'

The choices we make

We have navigated very different elements of courage in this chapter, from the small uncomfortable daily doses to the huge strides needed to take on difficult leadership roles. There is one more element in this discussion and that is when you, as a leader, need to make decisions that impact your life and possibly the lives of your family. These are the big, wrenching experiences that often come with the territory of working in very difficult conditions.

With more leadership roles offered to women, the opportunities are not just limited to certain sectors in developed countries, but opportunities emerge in developing countries, conflict zones where organizations still exist to serve and protect their markets. These appointments are not the same as glass cliff positions and, in reality, the risks are far greater where there is personal threat to a leader and possibly her family. The desire to take on these roles is aligned with a deep sense of purpose and commitment to catalyse change through their leadership, but there is no doubt these positions call for an extra dose of courage.

Kathy, a senior partner in financial services notes the following: 'I was asked by a male leader "How can you do this and be a mother?" And that's hurtful when you think about it, and on the same hand, "Well, you're a father and you're doing it, and nobody asked you about this!" So you need to have the courage to work along and deal with it. This comment was made 20 years ago, and I will never forget it! I think that finding the courage to be able to pursue your career path, even though you may hit obstacles and conflicts along the way, is clearly really important.'

Gwen Billon reflects on what she has seen over the years: 'A lot of women suffer from the imposter syndrome. They have been promoted to something they do not feel "capable of", and I had this syndrome when I was younger. But in order to progress professionally, you must step out of your comfort zone and take a leap of faith. I have noticed that the more people witnessed that I've stepped out of my comfort zone and succeeded, the more they wanted to give me more responsibilities. It evolves from a vicious to a virtuous circle. You must ask yourself how to define success and what you are aiming for. You must make sure you set out clear priorities and communicate with your manager, so you know what you are aiming for.'

Finally, **Delphine Inesta** shared a few words of wisdom: 'Do not waste your time by imagining things that people may think about you and being afraid. Only a teacher or a judge can judge you, and you are not at school or in court! You should take the opinion of people as advice and tools to progress, but not as judgements over your values.'

Sheikha Alanoud Al Thani, the Deputy Chief Executive Officer at QFC Authority, underscores the importance of courage in navigating the complexities of leadership and politics. In Chapter 5, she discusses the dynamics of workplace politics, emphasizing that a support system is invaluable: 'For individuals driven by purpose and a strong value system, the fear of manipulation diminishes. By fostering transparent relationships and relying on a network of support, one can gain access to honest, unbiased advice, empowering people to make informed decisions despite the challenges posed by office politics.'

A final note on failure: courage and failure are complicated as the experience releases emotions of disappointment, frustration, possibly even anger. As you experience this cocktail of emotions you are also trying to make sense of the events emerging. One of the most powerful actions you can do is to step back and understand the pieces, ask questions with curiosity – not to assign blame but to understand. Give yourself mental and emotional space to step back and listen to your instinct. It can be easy to seek the advice of others, but, while valuable, this can also cloud your judgement with different perspectives.

TAKE THE LEAD!

Pivot your mindset.

What do you do when you experience failure?

How do you react? How do you make sense of the experience?

Who do you speak to? How do you decide?

Don't get caught in the blame game. Be honest with yourself – did you under-prepare, expect too much from others, not give enough clarification, underestimate the resources required?

Now you pivot into learning.

What did you need to do this differently? What would have yielded better outcomes? How can you be better prepared for the next project that has some degree of risk?

How have you been testing, trying ways out?

Be honest with yourself: how comfortable are you with embracing change?

Note: Be careful – not all 'new tasks' are stretch roles! How will you recognize the right stretch role for you?

When you take on a new role, what else do you need to consider?

Be intentional: how can you make sure you get the visibility and recognition that should go with it? This might be a case of saying no if the stretch assignment is actually not a stretch assignment but rather one of those 'housekeeping' tasks.

CHAPTER 4

Connections

Going back to our sailing analogy, connections act as winds, propelling you forward with nuanced views, opportunities, support and potentially fun along the way. Connection is more than the network and the number of people you have around you, it is about building relationships and the nuances around the depth and breadth of these relationships. In this chapter, we will review the importance of connections as a resource for your career – so you know why you need this, how you will use it and what your action plan is around this.

Talking about networking brings mixed reactions, and very often the women participating in our leadership programmes will admit they find networking events uncomfortable. However, the connections we hold are a critical resource in every aspect of our working lives. Historically, women are the weavers of the social connections in clans, tribes, families, societies. So why do we have this discomfort with the idea of networking?

The least intimidating or threatening way for women to think about connections and networks is to think of them in terms of partnerships. In the effectual entrepreneurship literature (Read et al, 2010), partnerships are an essential dimension of new venture creation. Partners bring new means to the entrepreneur: time, experience, money, connections and the like. While the importance of partnerships in the new venture creation value chain is not explicitly singled out in the effectuation literature, their pivotal role in the sustainability of ventures becomes clear when looking at the creation and growth of businesses. By understanding the nature and importance of partnerships, it is possible to help entrepreneurs decide on what, how, where or when to allocate their limited resources (including time) to what will have the greatest impact on the sustainability of the venture.

In this chapter we will be looking at:

- connections as a resource – do you have the resources needed? Do we have enough diversity in our tribes?
- curating your network for your future goals – what is your current network?
- crystallizing the value of your network – start moving from potential to action.

Identify the resources you need

As noted by **Lucie-Claire Vincent Ortiz**, who held senior roles and has a broad international experience growing businesses and building brands in the consumer packaged-goods industry: 'Earlier in my career, I didn't know how to do the networking, who should be the right audience or people I should be reaching out to and engaging with, to develop and cultivate solid relationships.

'Part of it was my lack of awareness of the importance of having a strong, diverse network, and the impact it can have in your career and in your life. It took me a while to realize this, and I experienced its biggest impact when I was in transition. Throughout my career I had developed good relationships but most of them were within the company where I have worked for many years. They were my colleagues based in different parts of the world, but after I left the company, I needed to have a strong external network, and I did not have it.

'This is when I realized the importance and priority of networking, and to intentionally focus on it. But a network is not built overnight, and it requires attention, dedication and nurturing. It is not just one meeting or call, it is built over time, cannot be forced; it is a two-way street, reciprocal, and the best network is when you build trust and respect and support people, and this takes time and commitment. Having a network that you can rely on is very fulfilling and a way to continue learning and become a better person and professional.

'Also, when you are a senior leader, it is lonely at the top, and sometimes it is necessary to get different perspectives – obviously without compromising any confidential aspect of the business – and having a strong network at the right level in the right areas can be very helpful.

'During the transition period I learnt a lot, and met wonderful people, including several who are close friends today.

'Nowadays, networking is something that comes naturally to me. I am meeting and talking to people all the time, from very diverse backgrounds, from different industries, groups, organizations, clubs, chambers, education institutions, private and public sector, and countries. This opens a lot of doors, creates collaboration, learning experiences, new friendships, new business relationships, and gives you the opportunity to reach out to share learnings, bounce ideas, and get different opinions and insights. Networking also helps to develop mentors' relationships and to build your own board of directors who can provide advice and a different perspective.

'Networking is part of my DNA, and I will not stop. It continues to be an enriching, enjoyable and fulfilling experience.'

The founder of Aidha, a social enterprise, **Sarah Mavrinac**, confirmed the point and shared that she had underestimated the importance of partnerships, seeing them instead as relationships that required more nurturing and time than she had time for.

This is where the problem lies for a number of women. We see networks and connections as dimensions that require a great amount of time, investing in them in the same way that we would invest in deep friendships and relationships.

It is important to make the distinction between networking and connecting. Networking is about knowing more people; connecting is about knowing people more. Think about this: when you launch a new project, have an idea you want to defend, you actively look for partners, sponsors, individuals who will help you deliver on your project or idea. Networks are the same, and many of the individuals you meet will become partners in other ventures or projects, some will remain connections, others will become friends.

Networking is about knowing more people…

… connecting is about knowing people more

A striking example followed a conference on women in leadership. One member of the audience, a woman, walked up to Shaheena to thank her for her inspirational speech. Another individual, a man, walked up, thanked her and asked her whether she could help him with a project he was working on and requested time for a meeting. Needless to say he walked away with some great introductions. Spotting opportunities and acting on them are essential, and while it feels uncomfortable and awkward, over time it really does become second nature.

Lucie-Claire Vincent Ortiz suggests the following advice on strengthening your connecting skills: 'You probably start with the closer people that you know, and the first thing is your own network, because you don't sometimes even look at your own network – but you have family, friends, or friends of friends. And you can start from there. And you ask them for time in person or not. Every time that you meet with someone, you ask them to introduce you to two people. You don't need to ask for anything else, just please connect me with two people you think it would be great for me to speak with, because we have similar backgrounds, similar interests, whatever. And then before you meet those two people, you do a little bit of research on their LinkedIn profile or something just to learn more about them. So when you talk to them, you know a little bit about them. And to those two people, you ask them to connect you to people. So if you start broadening, that's one way of doing it.

'The other one is to attend events which have topics you like; it doesn't have to be directly linked to your career, because, in fact, the broader you go the better. Because if you keep on working with the same type of groups, you keep on encountering the same people. At some point in time, you have to keep on expanding to different groups – for example, the Chamber of Commerce or industries or even social connections. It could be a group of people who like theatre, or opera or whatever. But it's like you start trying to connect in different venues. One of the most difficult things when you go into a location and an event where you don't know anyone is how do I join and start a conversation? But you just start there. And you say, "Hi, I just joined here. I am Lucie-Claire." And then people usually open the space for you to come in and you just follow the process.

'That's the initial part; the difficult part is to keep the connection open. Because once you make the connection, you need to make sure this is not a one-time thing. You need to nurture it. Either you schedule directly, "Oh, we should reconnect in the near future" – or if you know the person and their background, and you know they are interested in something, then you can reach out spontaneously – perhaps sharing an article you think they'd be interested in. That immediately keeps the relationship and then they answer back. And then from there, you can even keep notes on everyone you meet and keep track of what they're interested in.

'You can then build connections through mutual interests, developing the relationship and the closeness to the person. But this needs discipline and organization. Salespeople are great at building connections because they have a calendar, and they know when they have to meet their customer again. So if they meet a customer today, they already put in their calendar three, four or six weeks from now that they have to reach out again to the customer. If you follow this approach, you'll have a clear structure and will know when to reach out again, and what to say when you do.'

Connections provide us with social capital, resources we call upon for various reasons – advice, information, introductions. As our work and personal lives become ever more intertwined and we are facing even more demands on our deliverables, investing in our networks often falls into a nice-to-have rather than an imperative to support career aspirations.

In this chapter, we broaden the discussion beyond networking, to understanding how our connections and our community strengthen our social capital and the value this brings to our work, and why we need to get better at harnessing the value from these connections in a way that brings value to us without discomfort or a sense of exploitation.

This engagement with wider society and through our own networks is far more complex as we navigate physical and virtual networks, and overlapping work and personal connections.

Understanding why we build networks

Not every connection needs to be aligned with a purpose – but the resources invested in building and maintaining networks mean we need to understand how we move from relationships to actions. This is why the analogy with partnerships is important. As entrepreneurs, we partner with other individuals or organizations in the short run or the long term because our interests are aligned or complementary, because our vision is convincing, and because together, we are stronger.

Among the essential players in our constellation of networks and connections, mentors and sponsors play critical roles.

As noted by **Delphine Inesta**: 'The death of my mentor was my turning point, and also because I had no choice, so I had to be exposed. It was not about me. It was about the survival of the company we were working at, and what we all believed in. I had to build connections very quickly when I was sort of thrown into the realm of responsibilities. I know that reputation is fragile, and it takes a lot of time to build, and it can be destroyed very easily. I think it is more solid if we base those relations on real and authentic, genuine connections, based on sincerity and loyalty. This helps reduce the fragility of those connections, otherwise it is just based on image reputation and fragile success.'

Even without referring to death, by the time we decide we need to activate networks, it might be too late. Building and crafting the foundations of a network take time and energy and a sense of direction, even if the expected outcome is not clearly articulated. Sometimes, too, it is okay to build networks not quite knowing why the network might be useful, but simply out of curiosity.

How men and women build networks

There are differences in how men and women build networks and there are also gender differences in the effectiveness of these networks. We need to dig deeper to understand the reasons for the differences and understand how we leverage similarities to strengthen diverse connections. What does research say?

Creating and maintaining networks require an investment of resources, and in most cases this comes down to time. Working women who still hold the bulk of domestic responsibilities

– what Arlie Hochschild calls the 'second shift' – have limited time for extracurricular activities. Networking activities fall into this category – happening at the end of the day or during the weekends, demanding time away from caring for family members. The structural inequalities that lead to greater domestic demands on women inevitably mean they have less time and resources for networking, and so opportunities, to a large extent, materialize within the work context. This is a double-sided issue: clearly, strengthening networks within the workplace brings benefits and feeds into management styles, as we will discuss shortly. The women we met were adamant that time was the first hurdle. **Gwen Billon**, an investment banker in London, was very clear about this: 'Some people are good at networking and others more reluctant. In any case, it is important to keep networks alive and not assume that meeting people once will maintain a connection forever. But equally you must be conscious of time, and you cannot be running around to every networking opportunity. So, it is crucial to assess the value of specific networking opportunities.'

However, these networks are limited to the workplace and often curtailed by functions or management levels, creating opportunities to build ties with individuals who are largely quite similar to each other. Homophily is the term used to describe how we cluster to people like us; we feel comfortable with others who reflect key elements of us and stay within these groups.

Paul Lazarsfeld and Robert Merton differentiated between status and value homophily. Status homophily refers to inherent and acquired characteristics – for example, gender, age, ethnicity, religion, occupation and education. In contrast, value homophily describes how individuals connect with others where they have shared values, attitudes and beliefs overriding status differences. The nuances of homophily help us to understand how different similarities can be. With status homophily, our connections are based on shared social experiences or norms that we can relate to. Consider the starting point of women's networks in organizations; they begin as a group to create solidarity for women where there are very few opportunities for women to coalesce and share their challenges in the workplace.

The effective networks transition to a resource, such as an employee resource group (ERG) providing mentoring, coaching and solutions that support women navigating these difficulties and that should help with retention and career promotion. These resources are incredibly important to create shared platforms, but there are natural boundaries in terms of diverse experiences and different thinking – the opportunities to tap into cognitive diversity from these groups are quite limited. Within this category, research shows women are more likely to network with peers and subordinates, once again reinforcing shared experiences without having the opportunity to stretch their experiences or thinking (Greguletz, Diehl and Kreutzer, 2019).

In comparison, values homophily is far more subtle and requires a much deeper dive into personalities and relationships to successfully build and maintain these relationships. The basis of values homophily is a shared understanding of values, beliefs and attitudes. These connections go beyond shared religious or cultural practices, and are based on a deep understanding of the other person and vulnerability in sharing values and attitudes beyond a superficial connection. These relationships require resources of time, effort and energy. However, these are the connections that yield significant benefits in terms of cognitive diversity, generating new ideas, solutions and resources. Networks that are rich in diversity create new opportunities and have a higher social capital for participants. But these relationships take time and can be more complicated for women to access and develop.

Networks exist in a state of potential, rather than actualization, and this is particularly the case for women. Brokerage is an important element in activating networks, where connections are made to enable information flows that give value to important outcomes. In other words, the value of the network is activated when information from the connections yields tangible benefits for the players. Networks are not organization bound.

Evelyn Zhang and her colleagues' research team build on their work on gender differences in brokerage to argue that people who retain their old contacts once they have moved to a new position perform better than colleagues who don't. The ability to retain networks is an important asset for women, and things can get even better as women become stronger in asking for resources from their networks.

What do you want from your network?

This question never fails to elicit strong and opposing reactions from women. The spectrum of answers ranges from the value of the network as a critical resource to explicit discomfort in asking for something from these connections, with responses including shock at exploiting connections.

Why women push back on activating their networks may be due to a combination of factors, with some researchers arguing gendered modesty might be a reason. Gendered modesty is described by Greguletz (Greguletz, Diehl and Kreutzer, 2019) as the point where a woman's personal hesitation takes over their behaviour, and manifests in self-criticizing their ability to make valuable contributions to their networks, which in turn creates barriers in extracting value from their network for fear of not being able to reciprocate. Reciprocity is an essential element in maintaining networks, and we are very tuned in to whether our support in networks is reciprocated (Janjuha-Jivraj, 2003b).

The women we met were adamant that their networks needed to be nurtured and reciprocated. For example, **Aminata Kane**, a VP for Orange, mentioned: 'Years after your studies and working, you do necessarily have a big network as expected, but if you do not nurture your connections, you will be losing them.'

Several of the women we spoke with echoed this view; personal and friendship-based networks have immense power. Cultivating the connections means continuously checking in, engaging and sharing ideas. Without constant check-ins, you don't have connections; you just have a network of acquaintances or connections. It takes time and effort, and there are times where you just want to shut down because it's so busy, but the rewards are immense, and you don't always know where the connections lead.

Shaheena shared her own experiences of connections over her career. 'As a young lecturer I experienced career-altering opportunities when senior leaders invested in me and introduced me to their connections. Over time I learnt the value of bringing my strengths and enthusiasm into connections. A key learning for me has been not just passively receiving opportunities but giving, and often giving when I don't expect anything in return. Over time I have experienced the value of generosity when opportunities open up from my much wider, global connections. My ability to create authentic connections and bring people together is recognized as one of my key assets. I get such a thrill from making connections and seeing what emerges from those conversations, even when I am not in that country.'

Similarly, **Sarah**, a senior leader in Asia, was very clear: 'Friendly networks are powerful, especially if you use them right, and if you invest in them. There's no point knowing people if you're not going to continuously be in touch, engage and deal with them. Otherwise you don't have a network. Then it's just called acquaintances or people I know of. So I invest in my networks, but it's tiring. You reach a point where sometimes you just want to close your phone and not answer anyone. But it's worth it. In my experience, it's what helped me become who I am today.

'First, the exposure, the learnings, the connections – it's the power of networks where, for example, if I need help in a certain country, for a project, you will find those people, because they know you, they respect you and they will connect to you. So that becomes a network of networks. That's not from a political or woman or leadership perspective in terms of how you manage yourself. That's more of how you perform, how you leverage and how you have a strong network like a man, right? I travelled the world, and I needed those networks.' As more women move into global leadership roles, it is more important than ever to build and maintain international connections. It takes additional time and effort to ensure these connections remain relevant and the benefits are not always clear. But in an increasingly tight-knit world, your value is more than your local network; it is also the strength of how you can leverage international networks for opportunities.

TAKE THE LEAD!

What do you need?

Pick an area you'd like to focus on for this exercise and answer these questions.

Starting from your purpose, what are you trying to achieve? Who can help you with this? How would you know them? And then go back to these questions and see how you could identify and nurture these relationships.

Where do you think you have a gap? Are you sure this gap matters? Where do you put your energy in your connections?

Very often you want to work on your weaknesses but maybe you need to work on your strengths.

Network mapping: who do you know, in which sector?

Who do you nurture, who do you need to nurture, and who are you losing sight of? How can you remedy it? What do I need that person for? Who else do I know in this context?

Reciprocity: add some creativity here and share! Where can I help this person? Prepare what she could be looking for. Think about reciprocity. Have you done your research on them? What are they

---

interested in? Who could you introduce them to? Could you set yourself goals to aim at connecting people? Where do you see the value where people you know could connect? Being known as a connector will raise your own value.

Caveat: not every opportunity is good to take!

Designing a network of connections that support your north star

What is the optimum size of your network?

We carry our network as an abstract concept, stored as contacts on our phones or on social media. Of course, we do not hold all our connections as live hubs waiting to be activated – the size and scale of our network makes this almost impossible. The rise of technology and social media means it's commonplace to have thousands of connections, but how many of these connections are relationships and will provide us with the help or deeper-level information flows we need?

Professor Robin Dunbar at Oxford University carried out research arguing that the human brain can hold stable and social relationships with 150 people. Dunbar's number became popular in Malcolm Gladwell's book *The Tipping Point* to explain the optimal number of connections that help to build the profile of connectors or boundary spanners. What if you are like many others reading this book – could you look at your contacts list and challenge this number? Over time, this number has been challenged as our networks are highly contextual, dependent on where we live, where we work and our level of exposure to international regions.

Our network depends on the extent to which our society determines access to networks, whether we live in individualist or collectivist cultures, our age and level of engagement with social media and technology. In reality, we have a small group of people we engage with on a regular basis to fulfil different needs, personal and work-related. A very small group may address both areas. But when we flip our perspective and start thinking about how we utilize our network, we often need to get beyond our regular connections to dig deeper and see how our wider resources can amp up the value to help us reach our goals.

Boundary spanning

Creating a diverse network requires conscious attention – boundary spanning provides a way to introduce more variety into networks by crossing boundaries. Boundary spanning is an important tool for leaders to share information and enhance collaboration, and it starts with strengthening the value of your network, your social capital. Boundary spanning is the terminology used to describe how individuals create new relationships beyond their normal networks, and in doing so broker connections to exchange information (Friedman and Podolny, 1992). Boundary spanning is particularly effective as a bridging tool when you have access to different groups of networks, beyond work or personal connections. If we work on the premise that our networks will emerge from the origins of status homophily, then we look for individuals who are similar to us in other networks.

The research by Araújo-Pinzón and colleagues argues that women are more likely to utilize 'boundary management' approaches to leadership which facilitate boundary spanning and encourage vertical relationships. They argue that organizations with lower representation of women in senior leadership roles are less likely to have the infrastructure and culture to encourage boundary spanning and opportunities for women to diversify and strengthen their network. Of course, we do not mean to imply that women will interact only with women, and this is also worth noting. It is essential to consciously step out of your comfort zone and interact with individuals who do not mirror you based on gender, race, age or status.

Finding and connecting with people who are different takes time and a genuine interest in finding areas of similarities. Of course, we cannot engineer every aspect of networking – serendipity plays a role, as do chance meetings, particularly in our personal networks. So far, we have focused on connections emerging at work; however, we know our personal lives create rich and varied opportunities to introduce and strengthen new connections, increasing our ability for boundary spanning.

Critical changes in our lives form opportunities to make new connections – becoming a parent and the network associated with schools, taking up new hobbies that have a strong social element, moving to new countries and building communities, volunteering. These interactions may start from shared experiences but, without the work context, the conversations are more likely to dive deeper into connecting through shared values and attitudes, strengthening ties and creating more diverse information exchanges. Without the framework of regular work interventions there is a need to be more intentional in keeping these connections relevant. We'll talk about the impact of social media later in this chapter, but in any case, how do you keep connections relatively warm so they can be fired up when you need them?

Nurturing your network

Creating a scattergun approach to networks creates an interesting and quite chaotic network; but without the ties to keep information flows and build social capital, the bonds are likely to weaken and dissipate over time. As with so many aspects of this book, cultivating and maintaining a network is a resource and requires your investment of time and energy.

As with any investment, you need to be clear on your return on investment. Your responses are likely to range from person X can help me access promotion or opportunities in a new organization/sector/region to person Y is interesting and I'm not sure what the relationship will yield, but there is the potential for value in this relationship. As our careers become more squiggly, and new opportunities emerge with the growth of side hustle, it's useful to have networks that are more diverse and provide us with access to new groups and resources.

However, if you are building a network aimlessly, without clearly articulating why it matters, at best you build a group of connections that take time and effort to maintain without generating the benefit. As we have discussed earlier, the inability to articulate the value of the network is exacerbated for women due to hesitation in articulating their benefits to connections, and this is compounded with limited time for networking creating a vicious cycle where it's difficult to experience their contribution to their connections.

Nurturing a network takes time and effort

Whitney Gore, who works at Netflix, shared with us her experience: 'You must nurture networks such as with holiday cards or Christmas cards. I take the opportunity once a year to send out wishes to people and to remind them of our connection. LinkedIn is a great resource. It is a frequent reminder to check in with your network – how are you doing? You must not be afraid of not getting a response. Nurturing a network takes time and effort, but there are multiple ways to reach people within a busy life and even from across the world.'

Dominique, a senior banker in London, reflected on this: 'I am not sure how to explain that, but over the years I have learnt how to be bold. If I meet someone interesting, I will make a point of engaging with them, instead of ignoring the opportunity. In a social set-up, I think it is important to make it your goal. You should introduce yourself or find a way to make a connection, otherwise you have lost your opportunity.'

Jennifer Publicover's words resonated with us as well: 'When networking, I reflect on how I can help the other person. I believe both people should come out of a conversation with a feeling of value being added. After I have a conversation with someone about driving our business forward together, I regroup and plan how we can move forward. I don't lose sight of these conversations after I've had them. I am deliberate with how I follow up. I invest more time now than I used to following up. I am constantly thinking about how best to use my time and how I need to set priorities or how I am aligning my connections with people to those priorities. It is about being the connector of people.'

both people should come out of a conversation with a feeling of value being added

One way to curate networks effectively is to take an intentional and planned approach to networking: mapping your connections based on your current and future needs and identifying key resources of individuals who can help you. What is important for your plans, what resources do you need, what information do you need to move, and who can help achieve that move and/or provide the information?

Compound networking

Dominique shared with us a very practical example: 'I'm trying to link it with something I like, for example I love music and opera.' So that's what she does. She takes clients to music and opera, and she's met very interesting people. And it has led to real business opportunities.

This idea of compound networking is no different to playing golf, football or the masculine models of networking, but it presents a different way for women to think about networking.

Long-term models of networking largely follow masculine approaches to formal work-based networking; yet, as we discussed earlier, we are more likely to overlap between work and personal lives and finding ways to blend personal interests with networking opportunities strengthens bonds more quickly.

TAKE THE LEAD!

What prevents you from reaching out to those you've identified as the key stakeholders in your progression? What are your current attitudes related to networking?

Write these beliefs down, reflect on them and decide if they are valid and useful for you. What do you want to change in these statements? Do you want more time to build and maintain connections? Do you feel you need to strengthen the quality of connections and reinforce your value as part of a network? Are you overwhelmed and unsure where to start? What can you address and challenge?

Ask a friend how she or he would introduce you to someone new, listen for what they highlight and if it resonates, take inspiration from them and use it when introducing yourself. Our inner critic creates so much doubt; listening ourselves through the lens of someone we trust is powerful.

If you have the opportunity, identify three people who will be at the event, and prepare your introduction or your questions.

What would be the value for them? How would you approach them to talk about this project and find a collaborative way to have a win-win situation for both parties? If you can't do this, find a hook to have a follow-up conversation. If a hook doesn't appear, just be authentic and find a way to stay connected – the future holds so many opportunities to strengthen these relationships.

Crystallizing the value of your network: moving from potential to action

Create your plan

When talking to women about connecting, common responses range from indifference to strong push-back and a fear of being rejected. There are no specific rules about how many events you should attend, but we suggest attending an event that is out of your comfort zone, with participants you would not normally mingle with, at least once a month. Set the target of making new introductions, and if you can't provide connections, choose the next best options, share knowledge – articles or resources that you feel are relevant to the conversation.

Why is this so important? **Whitney Gore**, who works at Netflix, is very clear: 'A lot of people often ask me, "Can you introduce me to this person, or can you put me through to a headhunter for this role?" While I think it is important to do this when you can, you cannot say yes to everyone because who you recommend is also a reflection of you. It can be difficult because you do want to get to know someone and have a relationship with them before putting them forward. So, to the extent I have worked with people or had the opportunity to get to know someone who has really impressed me, I have put them forward. I will make the connection and after that it is up to them. People want to be able to recommend you or introduce you to their own network, so make it easy for them – they need to know what you are looking for and why, so that they can express this concisely themselves.'

Joy Mpofu, an ex-banker who is now launching a femtech company, reflected on the power of networks: 'When I left the corporate world for entrepreneurship, I similarly valued connections and networks. In this case it was about people's affinity in believing that you can do what you are saying you will do. One thing that I will always be clear on is that your network is everything.'

Become a connector

One of the most powerful outcomes from Gladwell's book was the importance of connectors. In a network, connectors are the individuals who engage in expanding boundaries – reaching out and forming new connections, and also widening the networks of others by sharing these connections. Social media has made our relationships more transparent than ever before. As a connector you need trust in the individuals you are connecting, and so these relationships have strong bonds and are more likely to have shared attitudes, which means that the individuals will respect the relationships. Being a connector is not a zero-sum game, you are not giving away your connections, and your network relationships will not diminish because you introduce new people to each other. As long as your value in the network is strong and you are confident in what that value holds, then sharing your connections elevates you to the position of connector, someone who spans boundaries not just for themselves but for others. In our hyper-connected world of social media, the role of connector has a particularly important status.

Being a connector is not a zero-sum game

While some may argue that certain individuals are natural networkers, it is a skill and can be learnt. Much like taking an intentional approach to cultivating a network, the same approach can be adopted for connectors. Connecting means having your top connections at your fingertips and knowing they will reciprocate the introduction. This relies on keeping your network active and warm and staying up to date with movements in your groups. The immense value of being a connector means you have the opportunity to tap into vastly different networks, challenging notions of homophily and creating wide diversity that in turn provides you with strong social capital to become an asset, whether you are seeking information for new ideas or accessing different contacts for career pivots and opportunities.

Shaheena benefited first-hand from working with a prolific networker who went out of her way to provide introductions and connections. In doing so, Shaheena shifted from seeing the value of the network in what she got out of the connection towards strengthening her value as a connector. She knows her network is only as strong as the activity among her connections and constantly updates and introduces new connections.

Practical circumstances: working from home

We know the research talks about women being more invisible and losing the water-cooler moments. You need to raise your visibility, maintain your visibility in the workplace and in your working environment so that you get the benefits of working from home while still being visible. Post-Covid, people have realized that you can work from home and sometimes be more efficient at home, but this is also a balancing act. To build your network, you need to be in the office from time to time, but with an intent and purpose – this means not coming to the office and closing the door to be on Zoom calls, but proactively talking to all stakeholders in person.

If you are in the office three days a week, consciously use some of that time to network and strengthen your visibility. The heavy work that demands solitude and concentration can be done when you are not sacrificing networking opportunities. When you go into the office, set up meetings, breakfasts, lunches and dinners, especially if you are travelling. Keep space in your diary for opportunistic meetings and coffees. If you want to meet a colleague, use a connector to facilitate an introduction and request a coffee.

Cecile Hillary, a senior banker, reflects on the changes since Covid: 'Hybrid working post-Covid helps everybody, as well as part-time work, job-share, taking parental leave and sabbaticals. I think it is super important and it will make a big difference for women. However, women still need to be in the office and meet people, the face-to-face is still absolutely critical. When you are there, go to new people and talk to them – use all opportunities to meet people.'

Practical circumstances: in-person conferences

An important point about networking is what happens during in-person conferences. The real value happens during a few key points – whether you are a speaker or a participant, use the apps to find delegates and connect with them in advance, and as a speaker, invite participants to speak with you during the breaks. If you aren't speaking, then be ready with a question that stimulates curiosity from other participants so they will seek you out to continue the discussion. This is not to be confused with using questions as an opportunity for a mini-pitch, which is commonly seen as off-putting.

When joining a group, listen to the tone and then jump in – you are less likely to be invited to share your views, but keep your opinions clear, confident and concise. Offer to follow up with resources.

Once, at an energy conference in London, **Claire**, one of our participants shared an experience; she didn't want to be the first one in the main plenary room as she wanted to take time to speak to a group of men before the plenary session and they mistook her for an administrator or the person trying to usher everybody into the room. The real conversation starts from these informal connections in the corridors. So throw away the mindset that you've got to be the first one sitting in the front row during the plenary session, and instead be more divergent or rebellious. And be very intentional about your time and why you are at that conference.

Be creative and innovate

Claire was working for an oil and gas company and thinking about her next steps, and not sure where to start, but felt she was ready for a big change. Her friend invited a few friends who had transitioned from sectors, from countries, and decided to organize a dinner so they could meet and discuss. Claire remembers: 'The first dinner was at the Shard, with beautiful views over London – we had been given an alcove and started the discussion, which was so lively that we forgot to order!' The gathering was diverse, with new entrepreneurs, and individuals going through huge career changes. What was different from a sociable gathering of friends was the focus on problem-solving. The event became a series of dinners and virtual sessions providing everyone with a sounding board for their dilemmas and challenges. Claire shares the impact of that first event: 'Ten years later, what started as a solution to solve my problem – helping me figure out what my next step could be – became a great network and a safe place for kind and insightful feedback on our career paths and decisions.'

TAKE THE LEAD!

Manage your network of connections so you can call on them when you need them.

How often do you connect with your network? How do you prioritize and focus on the outcome?

Come back with 15–20 business contacts. Who do I have time to have a coffee with within the next few weeks or months?

Gratitude: saying thank you is a leadership style.

How do you use personal milestones to stay in touch? Farewell emails?

Conclusion

Mixed networks are invaluable. In some parts of the world, cultural constraints can make it more challenging for men and women to network with each other. It is never impossible, but norms can create additional barriers. As a woman, find male allies among your colleagues, or even among your family in communities with heavily networked, extended families. Be clear about what you want from your allies and enlist their support to help widen your network. Again, be prepared to reciprocate in strengthening their network as well. Time and again we assume others know what we want, and we forget to ask. No one in our network is a mind reader – you don't ask, you don't get.

connections act as favourable winds, propelling you forward

As we have already mentioned, navigating one's career is much like sailing uncharted waters. Just as a sailor relies on the synergy of wind, tide and charted maps to steer their ship, so too does one's career benefit from the power of meaningful connections. These connections act as favourable winds, propelling you forward with insights, opportunities and guidance. Among them, some will become your champions – helping you avoid reefs of uncertainty and find the most promising channels. This will be our Chapter 5, our fifth C: Championing. Just as a skilled sailor can navigate rough seas with the right crew, a network of strong connections can help you weather challenges and set your career on a course towards success. This will be our Chapter 6, our sixth C: Curating your team.

CHAPTER 5

Championing

Champions are necessary to promote career progression and will remain a critical resource until organizations address institutional barriers impacting opportunities for women. In this chapter we discuss how championing provides the catalyst for career development for women, and what you need to have in place to benefit from championing. Going back to our boat analogy, shall we say the champions are the guiding light of the beacons in the roughest sea? They might help you steer clear of the obstacles and could illuminate your path and advocate for your growth!

In many cases, championing comes from good leadership, when leaders care for their teams, invest in developing their career progression and spotting opportunities to further strengthen and nurture talented individuals around them. Championing is incredibly effective by virtue of the relationship that develops between senior leaders and talented individuals. When leaders challenge traditional approaches to connections and create championing relationships, they forge leadership routes that would otherwise be inaccessible and also develop a greater understanding of how diverse teams think, feel and behave. Shaheena's research led to the book she co-authored with Kitty Chisholm on championing women leaders, where they identified key components of championing talented individuals, the ones to watch (OTW):

- A senior leader can see the potential in OTW often before they see it for themselves.
- A champion can influence colleagues to provide opportunities for the OTW.
- A champion is committed to the career progression for the OTW in a way that supports their well-being.
- The championing relationship is based on merit and track record.

As you read through the list, you may be fortunate to have had someone who is a champion for you, someone who ticks these boxes. If so, congratulations and keep reading – sooner rather than later you may become a champion for those coming up behind you. In many cases, however, leaders may not understand the value of championing. In this chapter we will explore understanding the championing concept, building a brand for championing and creating the conditions for success.

Many informal championing relationships seem to be serendipitous exchanges. The experience of **Kathy**, who works in financial services, seems to be a chance conversation, but the intention behind the partner's question is there: 'I recall walking down the corridors of our office one day, and one of the senior partners stopped me and asked, "Kathy, how are you doing?" So, I answered something along the lines of "I'm doing fine, I'm working on project XYZ...", at which point he cut me off and said, "No! I mean how is your career going?" That stopped me in my tracks, and I never forgot the interaction. We found time, and he then sat down with me and helped me map out my next steps.'

Delphine Inesta, who works in the restructuring sector in Paris, reflects on these relationships: 'I identify my champions as those who told me, "I am going to give you this role and I am going to trust you for doing it and I am sure you are going to be able to do it." If I had the choice, I would never have trusted myself enough to do it! So, it comes back to luck and to meeting the right people who will be able to let you know that you can do it.' Luck plays a part, but knowing how you want your champion to support you is a key driver in how you identify and develop the relationship. Before we dive into the details, let's start at the beginning and clarify terminology.

Despite the importance of championing for women's careers, in practice it is still quite sporadic. Among the women we surveyed, 39 per cent did not have a champion. Just under half, 45 per cent, identified their champion as their boss. Champions are more effective when they are not your direct line manager, but someone who sits at a more senior level and can leverage their status to support your career progression. Therefore, only 15 per cent of the women we surveyed had a champion in a manner that would be effective for their careers.

Why do we emphasize champions rather than mentors or coaches? Understanding the terminology is important, and each of these resources provides important support for women with a particular outcome. The landscape for navigating women's careers and their access to positions of senior leadership is complex and it is unrealistic to consider that only one of these resources can pave the way.

Coaching: the International Coaching Federation (ICF) defines coaching as partnering with clients in a thought-provoking and creative process that inspires them to maximize their personal and professional potential. The process of coaching often unlocks previously untapped sources of imagination, productivity and leadership. Coaching is self-directed and focuses on self-improvement; it is immensely valuable when individuals know they want to achieve more but feel stuck and unable to identify how to move forward. Coaching is a time-bound relationship that is paid and therefore transactional.

Mentoring: the European Mentoring and Coaching Council (EMCC) definition of mentoring is as follows: 'Mentoring is a learning relationship, involving the sharing of skills, knowledge and expertise between a mentor and mentee through developmental conversations, experience sharing and role modelling. The relationship may cover a wide variety of contexts and is an inclusive two-way partnership for mutual learning that values differences.' Many organizations provide mentoring as a resource, which is a great start to supporting career development for women. Developing mentor networks is relatively cheap and efficient because the work is pro bono and typically offered internally across departments or even across levels. It can be significant in terms of time requirements for individuals who take on mentoring roles.

Mentoring is more likely to occur in cultures with a low-power distance culture. In other words, it works well in societies and organizations where individualism is highly valued and where there is resistance to strong hierarchies. The culture of an organization may reflect elements of the dominant culture of its society. You can see the impact in global organizations that have a strong culture but still need to adapt to local forces. Mentoring initiatives work particularly well in most European countries and the US. In these environments, mentoring is more common as the boundaries across leadership levels are more fluid and it is easier for middle management to have more open conversations with senior leadership.

Mentoring can be a hugely powerful resource to provide reflective practice and support women to solve specific challenges in their leadership journeys, but it is not a route for career progression. Mentors typically do not have the resources to support promotion and won't have the ability to determine career decisions. Mentoring is a powerful resource as a sounding board, but it needs to be recognized that mentoring has constraints when it comes to career progression. **Gwen Billon**, a senior investment banker in London, shares her experiences: 'Over my career, I was part of several mentoring programmes, but rarely found them really helpful because you are paired up with someone you have never met before, and who is not necessarily the right fit for you. It was much more helpful to find people who you know share similar values and aspirations or people that have gone through the same experiences as you, as they will be much more valuable to you. I was mentored by people with a few more years of experience than me and who could share their experience. I now mentor younger women going up the ranks, because they are asking themselves the same question I asked myself.'

As discussed earlier, championing is a nuanced form of sponsorship, a more proactive approach from senior leaders who take responsibility for identifying stretch roles that support career opportunities, particularly for women. The idea of championing and sponsorship has become widespread as an effective intervention to support women's careers. In contrast to *men are likely to* cultures that support mentoring, sponsorship is preferred in countries with a *promote mirror* high-power distance culture, where *images of themselves* inequalities and entrenched hierarchies are recognized. Despite the significant benefits of sponsorship and championing, our research reinforces work by Herminia Ibarra showing that women are under-sponsored and over-mentored.

What is the barrier that persists? Research from the Centre for Talent Innovation identified that 71 per cent of executives have protégés who are like them, in terms of gender and race. Research by Elena Greguletz and her team showed that women recognize homophily as a barrier to growth, but the structural barriers remain an obstacle to strengthening the diversity of their networks. The authors argue that, by contrast, men are likely to promote mirror images of themselves to 'fill vacant seats with clones'.

In Chapter 6, we discuss the impact of homophily influencing networks, and the same dynamics play out in mentoring. Mentors are willing to provide career advancement but don't feel sufficiently equipped to provide the appropriate level of support in terms of empathy and experiences to support individuals from different backgrounds. To shift the dial, championing needs to be a conscious effort on the part of leaders to strengthen the diversity of the population.

The barriers facing women are typically institutional barriers, which, when combined with self-limiting beliefs, can be catastrophic for their careers. Through our canvas, we address these elements by providing ways in which you can access resources and strengthen your confidence. Championing is an intervention that requires developing individual relationships, allowing you access to wider resources and opportunities.

How often have you heard of the Cinderella syndrome, also known as the tiara syndrome? These are women who are phenomenal team players, dedicated and reliable in getting the job done. Women who won't let the team down. Maybe you are one of these amazing individuals, someone who is a formidable team player. Someone who is so embedded in her team that she doesn't quite see her own potential, or someone who has been passed over for promotion, once, or even twice. The Cinderella syndrome describes how committed, driven women work hard within a team context, believing that their own performance will be recognized and rewarded. They are literally waiting for the glass slipper of promotion to be handed to them in recognition of their work and effort. Reality check – this doesn't happen often, if at all. Instead, they find they are constantly overlooked for stretch assignments or promotion.

The women we spoke with while writing this book, as well as those who have attended our leadership programmes, believe the same thing – that the quality of their work will speak for itself and that there is no need for additional help, nor any need to draw attention.

The reality is very different. Women need the voice of advocates to speak for them in meetings where talent promotion discussions are taking place. The men's club, boys' network, whatever terminology you choose to use, allows male leaders to identify opportunities and promote other men into these roles. Women typically don't have access to the same network, as discussed in Chapter 4. Decisions around recruitment and promotion for women are heavily skewed towards performance rather than potential – see Chapter 7. The barriers for women, behavioural and institutional, do not dissolve organically; conscious effort is required to change policies and behaviour.

conscious effort is required to change policies and behaviour

For championing to be effective, leaders need to set the intention to seek out diverse talent, ones to watch, from different backgrounds. The level of seniority of a champion is important; it must be an individual who has the authority to influence decisions around career opportunities. To address the gap in experiences, as discussed earlier in the mentoring section, the most effective championing routes cannot rely solely on goodwill, but require structured support to help champions understand their charges, who come from different experiences and backgrounds. Even more importantly, when championing is initiated with the specific intention to increase diversity in the leadership pipeline, and this is linked to performance appraisals, the activity becomes strategic and is executed with greater rigour. What you measure matters.

Joy Mpofu is today the CEO and co-founder of Flutter, an early stage VC-backed start-up, leveraging wearable technology, data and AI to unpack women's sexual experiences. She is a former VP in sustainability in a global investment bank, and spent the past decade in finance. Passionate about gender and race equality, Joy was recognized both within her former organization and leading industry bodies for her leadership and dedication to diversity and inclusion. Her success in banking was a combination of her credibility and performance, but she needed champions to amplify her visibility. 'One of my champions always told me that I needed to build a network. She told me that the bank was huge. I needed to speak to people and get to know the different roles. I approached these conversations with hesitation, as I didn't know what to expect from meeting with people I didn't know, but I quickly learnt the skill to build authentic connections. By having those conversations, within a year I had broadened my network, and built real relationships with colleagues that allowed me to work more effectively. When

I quickly learnt the skill to build authentic connections

I moved into another department, another woman in the division sat me down and described the industry – how the bank works, how to be visible, how to plan for my next promotion. It was valuable, as, growing up, I was taught to work hard to succeed, but in the corporate setting it is not just about working hard but also about how visible you are. Having someone to tell me that so early in my career was monumental. I was woken up to the structures of where I operated, and on top of that, she created opportunities for me within the division to be more visible. When I went to an event where I found someone more senior inspiring and I wanted to learn more about their career journey, I would reach out and ask to grab a coffee. I was able to build authentic relationships with a few managing directors within that department and the wider bank this way. Over time I had built a good rapport with senior people in my division that allowed me to be visible and also get advice on how to succeed in the department.'

Joy's experience demonstrates the transformative effect of championing when an individual finds the right support and recognizes the need to take responsibility to accelerate their career. A champion cannot address all the gaps for OTW; it is incumbent on the individual to catalyse the resources they need – for example, strengthening the network, as Joy did. In our research we found women expected their champions to do the heavy lifting for building networks and connections. There was an assumption that when they had a senior leader as a champion, the OTW did not need to strengthen their networking ability; this applied to internal and external networks. Having a champion is not a substitute for connections, but instead should be super-boosting your resources.

Championing is a structured activity based on strength and consistency in your capabilities, your experience and accumulated knowledge in your field, your competences. There are important elements to implementing effective championing:

- Your career aspirations, the clearer the better – even if you don't have all the details.
- Identifying a champion.
- Sustaining your championing relationship.

Your leadership canvas helps you to focus on your route ahead for your leadership journey. And as you develop a better understanding of your strengths it becomes easier for you to articulate why others need to pay attention to you and your work. The goal of working with a champion who helps you navigate your career path is to help you identify potential career paths, encourage you to take on roles that stretch you and encourage you to raise your aspirations. The value of a champion is someone who supports you, believes in you and helps you to prepare for bigger, bolder goals. You need to be ready for the challenge, but you do not need the finished product. However, the more you focus and refine, the easier it is for your champion to navigate a path with you. One champion may not be enough – creating a team that covers different bases is where you see serious results.

And as **Sheikha Alanoud Al Thani** shares, creating a team of champions who bring diverse perspectives is advantageous when working through challenging situations: 'This is where you need to have a diversified portfolio when it comes to champions, because you're not the only person on anyone's mind. You're no longer a kid where you need mentorship and continuous feeding of how you should deal with your environment. I've learnt now that I need to have multiple champions outside my work environment and the industry I work in. I need to learn how to be patient. I'm not patient. I've learnt to develop strategies when I faced challenges; who do I talk to for advice before I take any action? Of course, I can speak to my boss, but I need a range of advice. I speak to three or four different people, men and women. Women gave me different advice, which is very eye-opening for me because it's important, especially if you're dealing with men, you need to understand how they think. This is when I realized that your champions shouldn't be one or two similar people. And they should be people who are supportive and can be objective in how they give you feedback. You have other people who support you emotionally.'

Women are notoriously bad at advocating for themselves, but brilliant at doing it for others. Imposter syndrome may be a reason and we will come back to this later in the chapter. But essentially, as we discussed in the Compass chapter, women will push themselves forward when their leadership is aligned with a clear sense of purpose. They are less likely to promote themselves for the sake of their job or leadership. As we have discussed, paradoxically, hard work does not translate to promotions and the hesitation demonstrated by women can be misinterpreted as ambivalence or lack of ambition. If women do not trust the system, they are less likely to put themselves forward for stretch roles or promotions. Ambiguity creates more barriers to career opportunities for women than imposter syndrome. Women need to trust the system to risk putting themselves forward and it is the role of senior leaders to create a culture women trust.

Kathy Michaels, who is a partner at PricewaterhouseCoopers (PwC) in the US and has over 30 years of experience working with tax professionals, explains how champions have made a difference to her career: 'Championing is so important. Getting into a senior leadership role does not happen by someone alone. They get to that position by having incredible teams. Someone is looking after them – in meetings, raising their name, bringing their credentials forward. Everybody needs this support and I do not think it is very intuitive to people. You don't just find them; you need to be aware that you need them and so you do have to seek them out. But I think it must be a natural alignment in some way. And somebody that takes an interest in you. I think back to examples I had along my career, of people who were asking me how I was thinking about the future and making me think so much more broadly and strategically. And at that stage I hadn't really thought about that. The partner who then became my champion mentioned I was on succession plans for different projects, which I had no idea about. It was a pivotal time for me, because then we talked about how you go after that desire. He became really invaluable to me because he took an interest in me, he shared with me his perspective and what he knew, and helped me develop a plan to achieve it. Some people wait for things to happen, some wonder what just happened, and others make things happen. It may be women tend to wait to be picked and that's why having a champion is so important.'

Eleri J Dixon, who worked in a number of financial institutions in the US, told us: 'Ironically, when I signed up for the mentor programme in my company, they said, "You will be a great mentor!" I did not want to be a mentor but rather have a mentor, as no one in the company I was in had taken this role for me. They assigned me to a senior guy who was amazing. He did a lot of research about what was being said about me behind my back and what my reputation was. Without even trying, by the end of that year, I had a new job which changed the trajectory of my career at that company.'

Building a brand for championing: what's needed?

Championing is a relationship, and, as with any relationship, it's a commitment which comes with complex requirements and dynamics. As a one to watch (OTW), preparing for the championing relationship requires the same preparation as that required for career progression: a strong brand that is consistent, reliable and visible. Developing a brand may raise the ick factor, discomfort in self-promotion. Think back to the Cinderella syndrome – if you are seen as a team player, you are not regarded as a leader. As you shift gears for leadership, it is imperative that you create a brand that speaks to your leadership plans. If you are in doubt about the need to do this, then remember, if you aren't carving out your brand, others are doing it for you.

Championing begins with empathy, and it blossoms with trust

Kshama Pradhan currently heads BP's India Digital Hub for Innovation and Engineering – she describes how championing came at a critical point in her professional life: 'I have been fortunate to have good champions on multiple occasions in my career, in tough moments such as my twin pregnancy. The first situation where I had a great champion was my pregnancy. When maternity leave was granted for three months, I had to ask for additional maternity leave of nine months with the twins. While I was struggling to get it approved from other parts of the organization, my manager stood firm – having my back. He was appreciative of my contribution prior to maternity leave. He was also willing to offer me a bigger role on my return. These behaviours have always been very reassuring for me. Championing begins with empathy, and it blossoms with trust, and I was fortunate to be able to build these kinds of relations where I was championed. To inspire women, it is key to be championed. We all need champions, be it men or women. Creating opportunities for women to play multiple roles and encouraging them to pick up challenging work gives them the confidence to move forward. Often women do not find time for self-learning as much as men do. Therefore, it becomes essential to really focus on how you create those opportunities on the job for women to learn.'

TAKE THE LEAD!

What is your branding?

Key stages in building a brand:

1 **Start with your values.**
   Your compass matters. What you stand for, why you do the work you do. What makes you proud? The discussion in the Compass chapter provides the starting point for you to take time and think about your values. How do others describe your values/ethics?

2 **Your impact.**
   This is possibly one of the most difficult areas to work on – working hard doesn't equate with effectiveness or impact. The name of the game is about getting strategic when it comes to your work. How do others talk about your impact today? Does it align with how you want others to see you, today and in the next five years?

   Impact gap: Where are you now? Where do you want to be? What do you need to get there? Where are the barriers for you?

   Remember: your impact needs to be consistent to maintain your brand.

3 **Your visibility.**
   In the organization?
   In your sector?
   What is your sphere of influence?
   Who do you need to reach?
   How often are you interacting: touch points?

What is a champion looking for?

M B Christie has a strong track record of leadership in the digital sector, with C-suite and board positions; she is non-executive director (NED) for Moneysupermarket Group, a FTSE 250 listed business, and NED for organizations supporting social finance and tech-based entrepreneurs. As a leader, she is clear on what she looks for when championing talent: 'I look for positive energy and optimism – the kind of person who has the gift of making lemonade out of lemons. I look for curiosity, drive, enthusiasm and a sense of humour. I suppose underneath it all, I'm looking for resilience. My grandmother always said I am a survivor who keeps getting back up. I'm looking for fellow survivors.'

Creating conditions for success: allies and champions

Identifying a champion is the beginning of the relationship. The basis of successful championing relies on the principles of successful relationships, shared values, behaviours and goals. The pool of champions available to you is only as strong as your network. The first option will be senior leaders in your organization, these are the ones who can have a direct impact on your next career move. But real power occurs as you build a diverse pool of individuals who can work with you in different forms, support your development and nurture your potential while also advocating for you to access different opportunities.

Be curious, ask the question, take notes, do your research

Champions will only commit to you when there is a clear sense of trust in the relationship, and they recognize your potential. If you worry about the practical or awkward social aspect of talking to someone, don't forget **Karen Woodham**'s advice: 'Senior people are more than willing to give you their time, the benefit of their experience and expertise, if you show you are interested and approach them in the right way. Ask them for a coffee/catch-up! Be curious, ask the question, take notes, do your research, and if you still don't understand or have the answer you were seeking, go back and clarify, show them you have listened, but ask if they could give more background or context.'

TAKE THE LEAD!

The best way to move forward is to take a sheet of paper and write down the names of all your stakeholders, around your name, and start from there. Then for each stakeholder, question the professional relationship:

- Do they know me?
- Do they know what I do?
- Would they be able to explain what I do?
- Would they support me in a public forum?
- What information might they need to advocate for me?
- When will I next speak to them?

If I have answered no to any of these questions, what are the steps I can take to address this?

Then, in the relationship graph, you can start writing on the paper with some symbols, like a double bold line for very strong relationships, a single line for professional relationships, and maybe curved lines for relationships that could be stronger, so you get a sense of the strength of your relationships.

What does a champion do?

- Identify opportunities – in terms of stretch roles. Not every opportunity is right for you, but with the help of a champion you can determine which ones are appropriate for your skill set. Champions will sift through opportunities that bring benefit to the OTW as well as the organization.

- Understand how to prepare the OTW for the stretch role and recognize that the hesitation women express is not ambivalence but instead concerns and overthinking as to whether they have the required skills. The champion recognizes that a stretch role develops skills and takes the OTW out of their comfort zone – their role is to position the opportunity as a chance for growth and to mitigate risk or ambiguity.
- Strengthen the network for the OTW – provide opportunities for introductions that will strengthen their connections. These are individuals in the organization as well as those in the industry. This external connection not only validates the championing process but also helps to build the social capital of the OTW, which, as discussed in the Connections chapter, is weaker than in male networks.
- Provide constructive feed-forward – honesty must be at the centre of the relationship. Champions have a responsibility to provide perspectives on appraisals or how others view the OTW, strengths and areas for growth. Champions are working in an environment where they receive feedback an OTW will rarely receive directly. Unlike a line manager relationship, which is usually tied up with appraisals, the champion can provide input into areas that need development and opportunities to strengthen the brand and visibility of the OTW.
- Stay the course – going for stretch roles takes anyone out of their comfort zone and there is a chance of rejection. A champion cannot guarantee success. Failing to achieve a role or opportunity is disappointing, of course, but a champion is also a critical resource to provide constructive support when things get derailed.

It goes without saying that a champion is well-regarded, respected and strategic. They are a leader who not only has a strong network and is influential but knows how to use these resources for the OTW. Introducing new talent to discussions is an art in negotiation, and work needs to happen in preparation for big meetings to ensure colleagues are familiar with the OTW. This socialization may be in person, but may also occur through conversations, where OTW are championed for the impact of their work. This is where your brand needs to be consistent with the messaging from your champion and your visibility needs to be strong.

A word for champions

Stepping into the role of a champion is easy but also fraught with challenges. As a leader, at some point you start paying attention to your legacy, not just in terms of what you do, but also your successors who are aligned with your vision and goals. The new language of leadership – co-creating, creativity and innovation – means each leader is tasked with creating stages that can be built on and supported to strengthen the innovative DNA in the organization. As the data shows, leadership unintentionally picks mentors, protégés and successors in their mould, so intentionally setting out an agenda where you nurture relationships with high-potential individuals who are different to you is crucial. Creating a relationship with someone who does not have shared life experiences and social-cultural reference points may seem daunting, particularly when you are concerned about the boundaries of acceptable conversations and the nuances of political correctness.

But setting trust and a willingness to learn about different experiences create greater enrichment for your leadership and success in the championing role. In the vast amount of work in the DE&I space, becoming a champion may seem like a drop in the ocean; in fact, this action is more powerful than you might imagine. W Brad Johnson and David Smith (2018) found that in organizations where men commit to gender inclusion programmes, these are likely to be three times more effective in making progress compared with organizations without male support. When you successfully navigate into difficult and sensitive conversations, it will be deeply uncomfortable but also highly informative and likely to have a profound effect on your leadership. There are some hurdles facing men who get involved in initiatives and by addressing them here you can access the support to be a source for change.

What if I face a backlash by becoming a champion? There is some evidence that when men step into roles to support power-sharing for women there is a backlash. This is handled by how the championing relationship is perceived; if it is seen as supporting favourites or choosing gender over meritocracy, then the initiative is doomed to fail. However, where championing is positioned as a strategic resource to support the pipeline for diverse talent and receives clear internal support then the likelihood of success is far greater. Don't put me on a pedestal. If you have taken the step to become a champion and possibly the first in your organization, then you may well be treated as nothing short of a celebrity. You're the first and you deserve the accolade, but remember you are standing on the shoulders of many leaders, and, in particular, women who have shouldered this work for decades. When you are acknowledged, share the rewards.

Conclusion

As a conclusion, Cecile and Rumina share their thoughts on the impact and importance of champions at work.

Cecile Hillary told us: 'Having the right manager at the right times is a key component. When you are being championed by men and woman, it is important to be a supportive woman and give back. My responsibilities are the same with the next generation. So, it is not just about women; we need diversity to help promote people who are not just women, but from a different ethnic and social origin, LGBTQ+, people with disabilities, etc. There are several ways to champion people; obviously, offering your time and mentoring is important. I think it can be done, too, with public speaking or organizing networks – being vocal about the championing culture around me. The more senior you become, the more people will really listen to what you say and will try to understand. In my area, from a cultural perspective and diversity, we are really trying to raise championing, and I think women need champions. They need male and female champions.'

Rumina Velshi, President and CEO of the Canadian Nuclear Safety Commission, explains how she supports career opportunities for women: 'I mentor numerous women – not anyone directly in my own organization, but more generally. At the CNSC, we hold regular succession-planning discussions with our executive and HR leadership teams. We must meet with all our leaders on a one-to-one basis and guide them with career planning – while discussing as a leadership team about different individuals in the organization and how we assess their potential. Next, we champion them so they get nurtured and developed to take on more senior positions. We launched a Women in STEM mentoring programme that grows successful mentoring relationships, providing education and tools to enable these relationships, and also evaluates the programme on an ongoing basis for improvement. We also have a coaching programme to help women's careers flourish at the CNSC.'

TAKE THE LEAD!

Fight the Cinderella syndrome!

Find out what initiatives are offered in your organization. If there is no formal programme then start identifying two or three champions who can support you. Remember, they need to be above your line manager and may be internal or external to your organization, but with the ability to influence others.

Be clear about what your want, arrange a time to meet and ask for help.

If you don't have access to a champion, use your connections to get introductions.

Go in with a plan, be willing to listen and flex, and ensure you have a follow-up conversation scheduled before you leave.

CHAPTER 6

Curating your team

When you decide to set sail, assembling a crew is essential. On a technical level you know the skills you need, but it's also about curating a team of people who have strengths that complement each other and the journey ahead. You are committing to a goal and the way forward, but also navigating through turbulence and uncertainty. As a leader you face one of two situations: either you build your crew, or you are assigned a team. In either case your job quickly becomes one of getting to understand the skills, personalities and dynamics of the group. The captain considers each crew member a vital sail, adjusting their positions to catch the winds of innovation and collaboration. Just as a well-balanced crew ensures a smooth voyage, a thoughtfully curated team enhances a leader's ability to navigate the complexities of their objective, steering through waters with shared purpose and unwavering determination.

In Chapter 1, we discussed how creative solutions require an understanding of the barriers and how to navigate them; as a leader your role is to strengthen this capacity among your team.

In this chapter we discuss your leadership through the following areas:

- General trends in leadership, emotional intelligence and the art of curating a team.
- Gender differences in leadership.
- The conditions you need to create to nurture creativity among teams.

General trends in leadership, emotional intelligence and the art of curating a team

Leadership is simple and deceptively complicated in equal measure. Leadership is about vision, setting a goal and getting others to follow your direction to achieve the desired outcome. The question is less about what leadership is and more about how you lead: why you do what you do. For your teams, these questions are essential. We live and work at a time where leadership is more nuanced than ever before, we can classify leadership based on behaviours, and there are thousands of research papers and books dedicated to this topic. Even with all the definitions, leadership will still vary based on the individual, their environment and their team. We provide an overview of leadership groups, and as you read it you will probably relate to the definitions, you will recognize times when you have exhibited each of these behaviours. Table 6.1 below summarizes key leadership trends and are the ones you are most likely to recognize. These definitions focus on how the relationship manifests between the leader and their teams.

As you read through this table, you will probably feel some elements resonate more strongly with you than others. If we look at these styles from the perspective of nurturing innovation and creativity then it's easy to identify which approaches are more closely aligned with these outcomes; transformational, democratic, delegative and servant leadership rank highly. What

TABLE 6.1   Summary of key leadership styles

Leadership trend	Definition
Transformational	You inspire your team to perform well by winning over their hearts and minds.
Delegative	You work with highly skilled autonomous individuals, you are low touch, letting the team get on with the work. This is often described as a laissez-faire approach.
Authoritative	You are the subject matter expert, but you work with colleagues to create followership based on your credibility.
Transactional	You have a clean approach to leadership with clear rewards and consequences. This approach is low on emotional engagement and emphasizes routines and processes as a framework for transactional behaviour.
Democratic/participative	You include team members in the decision-making process and demonstrate a willingness to share power. This approach is also referred to as participative leadership.
Servant	As a leader you prioritize the needs of others, your colleagues and/or your stakeholders. Your starting point is a foundation with strong values to support others. This is a leadership highly aligned with innovation and creativity.
Authoritarian	You lead in a tightly controlled hierarchical structure where you hold total decision-making power. This approach is more common when working with teams who are low-skilled, carrying out repetitive roles.

is consistent in these leadership styles is the agility in leadership. It's easy to lead from the front, set a course and move forward assuming everyone is falling into line and following you. The process of creativity, however, requires a much more fluid approach, which means you shift from being upfront to working alongside the team, and at times even leading from behind.

All these leadership styles carry a strong emotional component that plays out as leaders interact with their teams and peers. Most executives today are familiar with the concept of emotional intelligence and its importance in leadership; it was first introduced by Daniel Goleman in 1998. It is likely you are working with leaders who have long careers, who started at a time when the emphasis was on leadership qualities such as intelligence, determination, vision and grit. While these factors are the baseline to demonstrate competence in leadership, they are insufficient to achieve transformational leadership, which is critical in a complex world. Goleman's work on emotional intelligence emphasized the importance of emotional awareness, self-reflection and emotional regulation. When we focus attention on the experience of women as leaders, and women being led by men, emotional intelligence is particularly pertinent. **Gwen Billon**, an investment banker in London, shares her perspective: 'I try to raise awareness among the senior men's ranks about what it means to be a woman in investment banking – especially being a working mom. In the younger generation, I see both men and women wanting to pursue a career once having had children. They want to make it work on all fronts without anyone having to sacrifice their careers. It is very important that the current management generation really understands what it means and how they can practically support their teams. It is crucial that all criteria for promotion or the review process are fair and unbiased.'

In Chapter Five we discuss the importance of championing as an intervention to support women's career progression, but at this point it is also important to acknowledge women who are still in the minority as leaders in their organizations. Role models remain an important source of inspiration for future generations coming into organizations. Maintaining visibility is another area that requires effort but it essential to strengthen the pipeline and inspire more women to enter sectors, particularly ones that are still heavily male-dominated. Strengthening the profile of leaders is necessary, but can challenging, as Gwen describes: 'It is very difficult for women to find their own leadership style from that perspective, which is assertive enough, but not too aggressive. Catalysing change in your organization is very important to me. It can be very frustrating, especially in a large organization, as change does not happen overnight. It is about incremental steps and what you can control.'

In the post-pandemic environment, we have a greater focus on creating psychological safety across organizations. The waves of change organizations experience create stimuli for leaders to address new challenges using different ways of finding solutions.

Women bring different perspectives and increasingly different models of leadership, which create opportunities for new thinking. As **Kathy**, who works in financial services, explains: 'Generally speaking, what I often see is women being the change agents. I think it's more because we are not as comfortable at getting noticed, but know we have to take that next step. When you are developing something that will be innovative or something that creates positive momentum and change, whether it's better for the team, the client, the firm itself, whatever it might be. Getting that consensus and agreement to do that is important, as it relates to change. I would say what gets some of the things right is more empathy, and female leaders might have more empathy, and team members might be naturally attracted to people who have more empathy. And by having empathy, it may be that we set guidelines. For example, I used to always have rules of the road during what we call the "busy seasons" in our profession, when you often work from 8 am until 9, 10 or 11 pm, every day. I always say to my teams: "All right, let's set a curfew – we're going to set a curfew in the morning over coffee, we'll get together and we're going to say, let's set a curfew for tonight. We're not working beyond 8 pm." This way, everybody knows, they need to get done by 8 pm, because we're all going home today, which was, really, very helpful to people. So, making those small changes led to a good change in behaviour because people knew "We're leaving at this time and this means we have 12 hours and we're not just going to be here indefinitely, so we can focus on what really needs to be done and matters most." I think that's an example where the empathy around the team's mental and physical health leads to a very good result.'

Leaders leveraging on diversity require strong empathetic skills. Working with people who are different, to effectively create opportunities for collaboration and creativity, requires building trust and it means understanding the different perspectives of team members. **Catherine Clark** shares how she harnesses empathy for her leadership: 'I tried to lead from a place of empathy and kindness, while recognizing that I have a low tolerance level for laziness, excuses and people who I think are dismissive or unkind. I have had to work on that over time, because to be an effective leader, you must be able to understand that you are working with people who are not like you. It is our job to create an environment which allows people to thrive using their own abilities. The way I have learnt to be a better leader is through taking on leadership roles, because it is easy when you are not a leader to criticize how decisions are made. It is tougher when you are in a leadership role and you have to make those decisions, taking into account a whole variety of different needs, issues and crises.'

Marina, Senior MD in investment banking, is current Head of Investors' Relations at a FTSE100. When asked what the common characteristic of strong women she has met was, she mentioned that it was the drive to prove something (to themselves or others) and grit: 'I think that women in senior positions have a greater ability now, versus say a decade ago, to show more caring personality characteristics, which is great.'

In 1963, **Thoraya Ahmed Obaid** received the first scholarship from the Saudi government for a woman to study in the US. She then worked for the United Nations, and is the former Executive Director/Under-Secretary-General for the UN Population Fund and a former Shura (Consultative Council) member in Saudi Arabia. She reflected with us on her leadership style, linking it to courage and compassion: 'Throughout my professional life, I insisted on working in programmes that are field-focused – to meet people where they live, hear their stories, understand their pains and joys, and have them express the way they want change in their lives to take place. The leadership I worked hard to exemplify is a leadership that ensures people are empowered to change their own lives, by contesting what they regard as impacting them negatively and expanding what they regard as impacting them positively. Leadership is about creating safe space for individuals and communities to interact among themselves and with others in order to move to a better context for all, women and men, young and old. It is what is now called compassionate leadership. This leadership is about being courageous in putting oneself in the situation of others and deciding how one wants to be treated, and thus treat those concerned accordingly.'

Empathy does not mean blind agreement, but it creates the space for you to understand what motivates your colleagues and how they will behave – particularly when things become difficult. It would be great if every new team member came with a manual; instead, it requires your leadership skills to assess your colleagues, and take time to get to know them. No matter how enthusiastic you are about the team and your goals, give yourself space to develop an understanding of how they think, behave and feel. The perceptions you hold towards others will be influenced by the nature of the work and the environment you are in. If you have the luxury to spend time getting to know your team in calm conditions, then you have the opportunity to consider how you flex your leadership to get the best out of them. The reality for many leaders is you are propelled into this position while the boat is already sailing, and possibly handling stormy weather. You have limited time and resources to understand the team, and you also need to be aware of your own biases or filters in how you perceive others.

When getting to know people, what are your reference points? How do you make sense of new people? The explicit titles are your initial guides – job roles, organizational charts, budget holders all demonstrate flows of influence. However, the covert elements are even more important. Who holds soft power – in other words, who has the ear of key decision-makers? Who has influence with the team, motivates and facilitates actions with informal authority? How do colleagues interact with you, on their own and in larger groups? What is consistent and what is not? As we discuss in the Compass chapter, you rarely sit down and have coffee conversations around values, but think about the conversations that help you discern the connection between what people say and how they behave. One of the most powerful ways to learn is through listening, letting colleagues share their perspectives and reflections, rather than jumping in with your vision. As a leader, you probably have your vision under development, but you need to understand how your team will deploy it. It doesn't matter how well-mapped the route is, if the team aren't on-board your boat will drift aimlessly.

if the team aren't on-board your boat will drift aimlessly

Getting to know team members is an investment of time, but it pays off, as illustrated by **Helene Bouyer**, who founded her own luxury and lifestyle hospitality executive search firm after having worked in the hospitality industry all over the world: 'You have to break the routine of daily meetings with 15 people and try to get one-to-one meetings where you can bring something to the team. This is the moment I managed to have their loyalty as they felt that I am here for them and will not use them to reach my own success. When they see teamwork, they can give 100 per cent.

'I was the foreigner. I was not in my country. I had to adapt. I was not able to say this is the way we are going to do it, but rather how can we do it together, by being very respectful of their culture and their way of thinking. This forced me to develop my managerial skills, cross-cultural management, attentive to my new working environment, and move forward whatever the difficulties.'

Curating your team

If you can create your team and you have a specific focus on innovation, how does this impact your recruitment decisions? The basic blocks are skills, diversity and range of experience, but how do you determine creativity and openness to new thinking. As we discussed in the Creativity chapter, what people say and how they behave can be very different.

Kshama Pradhan, VP and Head of the India Digital Hub for Innovation and Engineering at BP, shares how she curates for innovation: 'My role is focused on growing our digital expertise and portfolio of technological solutions to advance the global energy transition. Bringing in curiosity as part of the DNA is extremely important to us. When we hire people – which is valuable to us – we assess to see how people bring in that aspect. Showing courage to ask the right questions, or being able to challenge what comes their way, becomes

What binds people together is a common purpose

the differentiator. Once you have hired the right people, you must keep ramping them up to speed on a continuous basis. Technology is constantly evolving, and this means we must keep pushing and learning more about the sector that we are working to advance. Versatility is important because my focus has always been on building a team of innovators. We have to build connected communities. It involves developing and cultivating strong relationships with customers, nurturing partnerships with universities, vendors and start-ups. We hire people who can really come up with ideas that can contribute to BP's ambition, and we are not afraid of taking things to the next level by learning and growing. We are all human beings with different traits – some are more collaborative by nature. If you are forming a team, you will have people from multiple diverse backgrounds, roles, qualifications and skills, coming together. We see a greater opportunity because of this diversity of thought that's brought to the table. What binds people together is a common purpose, and that is what makes a lot of difference.'

Cecile Wickstrom reinforced this message in the Creativity chapter when she mentioned: 'Recruit for curiosity and then the rest becomes easier!'

TAKE THE LEAD!

Consider your current team as you reflect on these questions:

When you first started working with your team – who were you drawn to?

Who in your team do you now enjoy spending time with?

How curious are you about your colleagues?

What can you share about your colleagues outside of their working roles?

How often do you sit with different colleagues during coffee or lunch breaks?

How diverse is your team? When recruiting, how do you encourage diversity in the team?

Gender does influence leadership styles

There are many similarities in how men and women lead and there are also many differences. The role of leadership is experiencing far more change than ever before, and the types of leaders are far more diverse than ever before. One style doesn't outweigh another, but the different approaches are important depending on the context and what needs to be achieved. Earlier we shared different approaches to leadership and a great deal of work has focused on how men and women exhibit different qualities of leadership. We need to understand how these differences merge to bring new leadership styles and values to organizations. We have matured beyond the idea of women fitting into the traditional models of leadership, trying to emulate male counterparts who held the roles for decades, if not centuries. It's important to tease out the differences and understand how these attitudes shape new models of leadership.

Before we start looking forward, we need a quick glance backwards to understand why some of the negative stereotypes around women's leadership pervade the discussion. One of the most influential approaches to gender-based leadership emerged from work by Alice Eagly and Mary Johannesen-Schmidt in 2001, in a study differentiating between male and female leadership. In this research, men were described using two main leadership styles: delegative (or laissez-faire) and transformational. In these approaches the leaders had a clear vision, but they were working in ways that empowered individuals. The men used a delegative approach and encouraged autonomy among their teams. Women by comparison emphasized a transactional approach to leadership, using rewards for completing work.

There are times when transactional leadership is necessary, but when it is adopted as a default leadership position for an individual then it indicates a lack of confidence in their abilities to command respect or inspire others to follow their lead. The research identified another behaviour that was more detrimental: women were more likely to procrastinate around decision-making. A leader who delays making decisions creates chaos, confusion and demotivation. They are no longer a leader. Procrastinating on decisions can be explained by the presence of stress, ambiguity around goals, lack of confidence in judgement. These factors are not gender-specific; however, when women are in the minority as leaders it is more likely that these elements are emphasized and adversely impact their performance. Over time, the research reinforces stereotypes around women's leadership, limiting the value associated with diversity leaders.

Over the last 20 years, leadership styles have changed and there is far more convergence on what makes effective leadership across genders. Women have taken the lead in developing innovative approaches to leadership styles and generating creative solutions to challenges. Creating a different leadership style also means adopting a position where you demonstrate different thinking, as described by **Tamara Box**: 'When you're the only woman in the room, you have unique experiences and opinions to offer, and you absolutely must use your "difference" to challenge conventional or conformist attitudes. Only you can do it, so don't hesitate to be disruptive. This outsider perspective is one of the undersold values of empowering and putting more women into various senior leadership roles, and enterprises are finding that their decision-making is enhanced by these extra questions, opinions and judgements. As even more under-represented groups make their way into boardrooms and C-suites, greater innovation, originality and improvement will result.'

This view is supported by **Susanne Thorning-Lund**, a partner in Odgers Berndtson Board Practice, supporting companies in the development of balanced, diverse and effective boards. Susanne reflects on the value of women in leadership positions: 'The ability to take a balanced, system-wide view is what will get you noticed – as well as delivering, of course. Being able to put yourself in your colleague's metaphorical shoes is not the same as unconditionally accepting or acquiescing – empathy and support are positive, but appropriate challenge is critical. After all, your experience and insights are what got you to the board level in the first place.'

The superpower of diverse teams lies in the culture set by you as the leader, to create conditions for people to feel safe to constructively challenge assumptions, question why processes follow a certain path, and create openings for colleagues to think differently. How do you do this as a leader?

Creating the conditions for leadership teams

Contrary to common belief, multicultural or global teams do not systematically perform better than local teams. Their performance is likely to be either a lot worse or a lot better than that of a national team. There are several reasons for this, which cannot be attributed only to cultural differences. While it is true that global teams need to work with greater diversity, even local teams are composed of individuals with different motivations, commitments and experiences. There is a greater potential for conflict in global teams, as individuals work around different assumptions linked to authority, the management of time or what it means to be a team member. But if the team can work around these differences, they bring together complementary knowledge, perspectives and assumptions, sometimes referred to as affective versus cognitive conflict.

A team does not exist until its members have built relationships. These relationships in turn cannot exist unless there have been face-to-face meetings, and a process by which the team members get to know each other. Global teams are often set up to solve complex problems under great time pressure. The team members need to trust each other and share a common context to work effectively together. This is often difficult – most people shy away from sensitive issues. Conflicts do not surface, and confrontation does not happen. As a result, members build only superficial relationships, and the team goes nowhere. With poor results, team members feel increasingly disengaged. As a leader it's essential to keep checking in with the team, to recognize how dynamics may impact delivery and then decide how to address the situation. Navigating allows leaders to step back and let the team resolve situations or know when to jump in and steer away from obstacles ahead.

It is impossible to discuss creativity and innovation without addressing diversity. Creating a team that is diverse takes time, but it is by no means the end result – instead, it is the beginning of the journey. However diversity is defined in your organization, gender is still a core element that needs to be addressed; progress exists but it can be erratic. Leading teams of diverse individuals is not a light-touch effort; everything we have discussed in this chapter is essential and needs constant tweaking in the forming stages of the team to create psychological safety to boost creativity and new ideas. Recruiting for diversity does not automatically yield these results; you need to invest in the team to nurture cognitive diversity, differences in thinking and perspectives to shape solutions. If you create a culture that requires team members to work hard to fit in, you are unintentionally blunting the value of diversity. This is what we call 'fault lines' – teams that split across diversities that were not factored in initially. When any sort of in-group/out-group dynamic emerges, this is aligned with a power struggle where the in-group has formal or informal power to dominate decision-making and exclude the value of diverse perspectives. Strong innovation and creativity require conflict, ideas clashing and being challenged to come up with new thinking and strong leadership, as described by **Kshama Pradhan**, Head of Innovation for BP India: 'There will be conflicts – which are healthy as they help people to open up and speak their mind. A leader's role is to see how they can convert these conflicts into opportunities and help people to confront each other, speak their mind, build an open and transparent culture where people do not feel hesitant, and, rather, connect better to the common vision. Storming is an essential element when forming a team – we cannot escape it. If we really expect teams to perform, then it is the journey that is important, and as a leader you must assist to turn it into a positive. There are two ways of looking at conflict: being a leader dealing with conflict in the team and being part of the conflict. There are two different dimensions. As a leader, when I must deal with a conflict, I think just being aware that there will be conflict as we form teams is important. Navigating through the process to make a win-win situation for the people who are in the conflict becomes *If we build trust within the relationships, it solves 50% of the problem* essential. It means encouraging people to confront, come together, let them speak, give the assurance that they can speak their mind. It is about being a sounding board. It helps because when you are authentic, people understand getting into their reflective space becomes very important.

'When I am in conflict, it is about reminding myself that I must step back from the situation into a reflective space, and just introspect about the entire situation. I believe that trust is a very important aspect. If we build trust within the relationships, it solves 50 per cent of the problem. The genuineness of the authenticity with which we have conversations meets the other half of it, because what we are debating about, or the conflict about this journey, matters. It is all about how you manage those relations with people and build trust so that you can take it to the other side.'

Recognizing that conflict is inevitable and can be channelled in a constructive way is important and invaluable for a leader. We spend a lot of time focusing on creating cultures of belonging, but this must be balanced with the inevitability of disagreements on why and how projects are led. As a leader, if you model a way to handle conflicts constructively you create confidence for others to disagree and not feel excluded or marginalized. Inclusion goes some way to helping this, but at its core it still relies on the premise that as long as you fall into line then you are valued. Adopting a more progressive approach through pluralism allows for every team member to feel comfortable and celebrated for their differences. Pluralism supports the leadership styles most closely associated with innovation and creativity: as discussed earlier, that is transformational and servant leadership. For pluralistic leadership to thrive, you need to be genuinely curious and interested in your colleagues and invest effort into getting to know them. You need to get past awkwardness and concerns around what is politically correct and ask questions that encourage more trust and open dialogue.

Elerli J Dixon, who has brought together global teams, shares how she leverages getting to know her team well: 'It is super lonely at the top. You must understand the DNA of the people who work for you and the people around you. You have to know enough to understand the DNA of a person. How are they bringing this to the table? It is going to show up in everything they do at the office? And you need to know how to manage it. If you form a team where there is good dialogue, you can actually be brought together because you do not all have the same skills, and because you are excellent at your skills. It is more of a recipe. I have had this success happen so many times when you start a dialogue and then you generate good conversation as you encourage them to share their ideas. So, I brought all these people together and I was able to hire a team to decide on something. We had space for disagreements and one time one of my respected partners said she did not agree on the way to proceed because of numerous reasons. I was so thankful she brought it forward – it was amazing. As a leader, you need to believe in yourself; there are a lot of insecure leaders. If you are insecure, then you do not offer that opportunity to make your team shine. The more I made my team shine, the more it lifted me up as they supported me. I have hired these people and have moulded or mentored them. With insecurity or organizations run by fear, you do not see that as much. In those organizations, you do not get the best out of your people because mistakes will happen.'

Teams and creativity: the innovation element

When it comes to creativity and innovation in teams, your people are your superpower, but you need to create the conditions for creativity to flourish, as we noted above. Creativity, as we discussed in the first chapter, is about developing your creative muscle, and doing the same for your teams and across the organization. What are the practical ways for you to strengthen creative confidence with your team? The structure of the organization and the team matters. Flatter structures are recognized as providing greater flows of information to support creativity. This does not mean, however, that hierarchical organizations do not generate creativity, but it is more challenging. Within hierarchies, creating pockets for creativity is particularly effective, as leadership encourages more open conversations and demonstrates different approaches. Innovation cannot be switched on and off, but if you are pioneering a more innovative approach to problem-solving, then start small, set parameters around how team members communicate with each other, build confidence in challenging each other, reinforce the benefits. As credibility grows you can diffuse these practices across your teams, department and throughout the organization – another example of joining the dots.

Creativity is a team sport

Creativity and innovation depend on new ideas, new ways of addressing problems and creating solutions. As a leader, what happens when you are seeking new ideas and ways of thinking, and proactively encouraging your colleagues to challenge assumptions and generate new ideas? If you have created the conditions for colleagues to consistently generate new ideas, then the creativity is firmly embedded, but if you find the creative strength is fledgling then there are areas you can address. Creativity is a team sport – when dealing with creativity, remember iteration is the key to success and the law of diminishing returns. If you extend the time it takes to launch an idea, you can miss market opportunities. Iterating, the practice associated with lean start-ups – putting forward ideas that are sufficiently developed, but not finalized – allows you to test the idea with your stakeholders and incrementally improve without missing the boat. This approach means being comfortable with the idea of acknowledging mistakes. The most powerful way to address this, as we discussed in Chapter 1, is by shifting the mindset of the organization into a learning environment, where mistakes provide stimuli for learning and improving on how things are done.

As we discussed in the creativity chapter, providing space for taking risks and failure is critical, but absorbing this behaviour into teams is far trickier when colleagues are worried about performance reviews and how they are perceived. Creating a culture where experimentation and innovation are valued, and occasional failure, is incredibly powerful, as described by **Whitney Gore:** 'Creativity is everywhere, and I certainly do not see it as a gender-associated skill. These days, we have much more representation of gender across the industry. There is diversity in writers, actors and, increasingly, directors. In the entertainment field, to bring something new to an audience on a screen, you have to be daring. Being creative is to be daring and I see women embracing this, such as Shonda Rhimes. As the legal partner to creatives, we also need to be innovative. We must be individuals who are not a product of legal's risk environment, but instead are willing to suggest something without being stopped by the reactions of habit.'

Nurturing creativity requires team commitment, it cannot occur just because the leader wants it. **Marie Planckaert** has the role of firing up innovation in a relatively stable environment, working with highly skilled scientists: 'I love it when I have people that are different, but thrive when working together. I want to make sure that I have a group that can work together, but also have as many people with as many viewpoints and experiences as possible. But to make the team thrive, I couldn't just go in and demand it. I usually ask my team to think and get involved on how we want to achieve the objective together and, often, to define what transformation project is needed to improve our way of working. I prefer to do that exercise outside the office, away from the day-to-day environment and often with a coach to build cohesion, trust and agree on these projects. Most of the people who were reluctant at first usually see the value of it.'

The importance of trust

Trust is arguably the most important dimension of leadership. In teams it plays out in several ways: trusting each other to deliver, trusting each other to provide a safety net if someone falls, trusting to share new ideas to drive creativity and break from boundaries. Trust is a small word for so much complexity and so great an impact. As a leader, you set the tone for your colleagues. How do you proactively articulate and demonstrate a culture of trust? How do you clearly set expectations about how you work, your role and your colleagues' expectations towards you? And, most importantly, do what you said you would do? How do you communicate with your team? How do you ensure you have the pulse of your colleagues? Are you aware of the mood, the motivation and energy levels? This is particularly difficult in hybrid and remote work environments, where you are deprived of the coffee corner and corridor chats. 'Spontaneous' conversations are difficult to create, and taking time for small talk appears a waste of time on video calls that are engineered for efficiency.

But there are ways in which you can be present, to create check-ins with colleagues. Trust is built with a constant drip. For your colleagues to feel comfortable challenging ideas, and bringing new ideas to the table, they need to have a sense of your reactions to quirkier ideas. When deadlines are tight, and your schedule is demanding, checking in with colleagues can seem like a luxury that can be put on the back burner – but it's even more important when things are tight.

When you are stretched, your team is likely to be in a similar position, experiencing the reverberations without the benefit of your vantage point. The current focus on burnout in the workplace is a testament to teams operating under significant pressure, high workload, unrealistic expectations coupled with insufficient support. As discussed in the chapter on creativity and innovation, perfectionism kills the dynamic in teams. As a leader, your skill is to balance the need for high performance with keeping your team strong and feeling supported. You cannot do this if you are overstretched and pressured. Your emotional state is highly contagious, in both the physical and the virtual space.

This is known as emotional contagion. The research around reactions to facial expressions is well-recognized from research dating back to the early 1960s. More recently, however, research has focused on how these reactions transfer emotions and the impact they have on the recipient (Herrando and Constantinider, 2021). As organizations become more aware of the role and impact of emotions in the workplace, leaders become even more focused on the importance of emotional regulation. We discussed the impact of emotions in leadership earlier in this chapter, and emotional regulation is essential to nurture trust.

As you build relationships with team members and understand your colleagues better, you are better able to adapt your approach to their needs. This doesn't suit everyone, but the evolution of the diversity agenda has demonstrated the importance of moving from treating everyone equally to adopting an equitable approach. Equitable leadership provides a platform where you understand your colleagues as individuals – their strengths and quirks – and you flex your leadership to get the best from your team. If this feels like hard work, remember the alternative is constantly building a new team, as attrition rates continue. If you genuinely aren't curious about your colleagues and interested in getting to know them, then it may be time to consider why you want to be a leader. Leadership is not a solo sport. Modelling strong leadership among your colleagues creates the foundation for your team members to replicate this behaviour. If you demonstrate a willingness to trust, delegate and let colleagues participate in the problem-solving process, and as they experience the benefits, it becomes safer for them to allow others to do the same.

'Do as I do not as I say.'

Think back to the earlier discussion on gender differences in leadership and the traits attributed to women, reciprocal benefits and procrastinating on decision-making – both elements are the default styles when trust is low. Signalling trust occurs in different ways, and much of the current conversation on hybrid working is about trust and how it is evident in different organizations.

Rumina Velshi works in a highly sensitive and tightly regulated environment and, as with many organizations, the pandemic required conversations on how to create more flexibility based on trust: 'During the pandemic, as a science evidence-based organization, we looked at what this future of our workplace would look like. We built a cross-functional horizontal team to make sure that we were looking at different perspectives, but in a thoughtful way with employee participation. Now, we give this flexibility to employees and let the teams decide where they want to work or how they want to work. We had a very comprehensive set of performance measures to monitor how we are doing. Being able to attract and retain top talent is huge – flexibility allowed us to do that. It is hard for a regulator to be competitive based on compensation within our sector. This flexibility, however, is something that we offer that others don't – and for women is of enormous importance. It involves greater participation of women in our workforce, less turnover, increased productivity rates.

'I believe providing this flexibility in the workplace, especially for women juggling career and family responsibilities, is imperative if, as a society, we want women to be able to take on leadership roles.

'Going to a hybrid workplace forced us to trust our employees more out of necessity. We needed to be thoughtful and clear around task assignments and expectations. Hence, people became better at delegating and monitoring. We initiated regular pulse surveys to assess the mood, rough points, issues, respect, trust and safe spaces.

'Our inclusivity model at the CNSC reinforces that it is acceptable to have different opinions, as long as we listen to each other and communicate with respect and no judgements. To create psychological safety as a leader in an organization is to be an example and put yourself out front and deal with a range of reactions. Part of this needs to remain a legacy, the culture really needs to be baked in, or it goes with the leader when you leave the company.'

Trust is one of the important elements in compass, particularly when you want others to trust your leadership approach and direction. Over the last decade, we have witnessed the erosion of the barrier between work and personal issues. Consider the range of topics organizations address through networking events, talks, research and training – sexual harassment, race inequalities, mental health and wellbeing, domestic violence, age-related health factors such as the menopause – these are just a few issues that have become implanted as part and parcel of workplace conversations, when they used to be confined to the private sphere. The pandemic and tidal wave of virtual meetings broke the barriers between work and home, and these issues have ensured personal aspects of employees' lives are increasingly recognized as valid conversations in the workplace. To feel comfortable blurring these areas means trusting the environment.

Leaders responding to the pace of change need to demonstrate credibility and develop trust with their colleagues to effectively respond to opportunities. This view is supported by **Susanne Thorning-Lund**, a partner in Odgers Berndtson Board Practice, helping companies in the development of balanced, diverse and effective boards. Susanne reflects on the value of women in leadership positions: 'The ability to take a balanced, system-wide view is what will get you noticed – as well as delivering, of course. Being able to put yourself in your colleague's shoes is not the *appropriate challenge is critical* same as unconditionally accepting or acquiescing – empathy and support are positive, but appropriate challenge is critical. After all, your experience and insights are what got you to board level in the first place.'

TAKE THE LEAD!

Who leads on creative ideas in your organization? How do they work with their teams?

How do you shift the culture towards creativity in your teams?

How can you find ways to reward effort rather than just end results?

How can you demonstrate creative thinking to your teams?

How can you provide safety for new ideas that may fail?

How do you shift the narrative from risk and failure to learning and creating?

Women leaders as levers for soft power

The way in which different groups access power is a clear indication of how marginalized groups navigate institutional structures. Hard power is easier to understand – formal authority legitimized through institutional roles, often clearly demonstrated in formal and hierarchical structures. Look at any organigram to understand reporting structures, directly and indirectly. In contrast, soft power is informal, navigating around structures and formalized leadership roles. This form of power emerges when the power of personality, aligned values or social/ political views are utilized to exert influence on others.

The impact may be power among peers but can extend across levels – downwards and even upwards. It is easy to see why soft power is more likely to thrive in networks that are homophily in their nature – we discuss this in the Connections chapter. Women are more likely to assert themselves using soft power when their access to traditional leadership structures has been restricted.

Aminata Kane shares her perspectives on how women leaders can help female colleagues access soft power to utilize the barriers they face: 'I get positive energy from promoting the inclusion of women, if it is meritocratic. You assume the baseline must be competence, but most times we do not start in the same place. There are things women do to hold women back and to hold themselves back. When we see roadblocks, or people holding women back for the wrong reasons, we need to call out and challenge these behaviours. On their end, women must say: I can be quite proactive about building a network and a community that is going to be supportive and yield results, and not be scared about asking for what I want. My purpose is twofold: to bring on the global stage positive stories about what is going on in Africa – the innovation, the drive, the resilience I witness day to day by living on the con-tinent; and to give women the opportunities they work hard for and deserve. I am now intentional about offering opportunities to women, and helping them to reduce their imposter syndrome.'

Rumina Velshi shares similar experiences with **Aminata**, being a woman and minority ethnic in a traditionally male-dominated sector. She, too, leveraged her position for women in the field: 'The big thing for me was gender equity in the nuclear sector, as it is not well-represented by any equity-seeking groups (women, ethnic minorities). It was very evident to me that the face of the nuclear sector needed to change given the aspirations and challenges that lay ahead. As the regulator, you have many avenues to influence your own organization, and more broadly the sector.

'Leadership roles can erode women's confidence, and this is when you hear about the imposter syndrome; I am not ready for this. It is the self-doubt that emerges because of gender roles. There will always be differences of opinion. People in my organization have a high level of expertise, and you must create the space for them to voice their different perspectives, opinions, without fear of reprisal and confidence that they have been listened to.'

As we draw together the main elements that nurture teams for innovation, let's focus on the top five points.

1 Creating teams does not automatically yield innovation – cultures for creativity and innovation are the result of consistent and conscious decisions to strengthen relationships.
2 Gender differences create opportunities for different perspectives; women and men have different leadership styles, all of which are equally important to support innovation in organizations.
3 Inclusion is a useful starting point, but it can stifle diverse thinking, creating a pluralistic culture where different perspectives are valued and encouraged to strengthen the calibre of thinking for problem-solving.

4 Trust is the cornerstone to support leadership for creativity and innovation; trust relationships require regular and consistent investment in your teams.

5 Women leaders are able to help female colleagues navigate barriers and access soft power to strengthen leadership opportunities.

TAKE THE LEAD!

How do you create white space for your team?

What does successful delegation look and feel like for me and my team?

How will you plan a meeting where colleagues are leading?

Can you consider rotating the chair of your meetings to redistribute the power base within your team?

CHAPTER 7

Career

We have progressed through 6 Cs – Creativity, Compass, Courage, Connections, Champions and Curating teams – and are now concentrating on our last C, Career. We have taken you on a voyage of 7 Cs (seven seas?), giving you opportunities to explore how each of these areas is essential to your leadership. You may be wondering why we decided to conclude with career, rather than position it at the beginning of this book.

In your career you need to address each of these areas and weave them together to navigate your route. Through our experiences of delivering programmes and coaching, we recognize that the encompassing work on career is better understood when women have had a chance to focus on various elements before, so they get a better sense of what they want to achieve. At this point you may have a clearly defined route and all the elements are falling into place and your canvas provides a clear way ahead. In contrast, for some of you, the route ahead is still hazy, you have a general sense of direction, intuitively you know what you are doing, why you are doing it, why you are drawn to certain roles, even if you can't articulate it yet. If you are in the latter group, then working through the areas in the canvas will help to clarify your thinking.

Continuing our sailing metaphor here, your career is the basis of your canvas, it provides the hull to your boat, with the strength to sail the seas, through calm waters and turbulent storms. The canvas was developed to help you map out what you need to consider as you visualize your career, what matters to you, where you want to go and the path to get there. It was built on the demonstrated principle that women often think more creatively about their careers, and problem-solve in new and wonderful ways.

When selecting the women to interview for this book, we chose individuals who had interesting stories around their careers. By collating such a rich and diverse group of women, we have created a group who demonstrate divergent examples of flourishing careers. During our interviews with women, we usually started the discussions around career and what career success meant for them. We had as many responses as we had women, but we could find commonalities – in particular, aligning their activities with a strong sense of purpose, challenging assumptions and strengthening their self-efficacy, setting goals and using their achievements as stepping stones for the next target. We will give you a chance to deep-dive into these quotes later in this chapter.

Connecting the dots

Turning to you – what does career success mean to you? Is it comfortable for you to describe? How much clarity do you have around success for your career? Understanding why you do what you do is important, but how often do you think about success and what this means for you? For your career? Many of us only understand purpose and success with hindsight.

How often do you have the opportunity to step back and survey your career? Perhaps when you are asked to give a speech and to share your story, you map out key points where you took decisions that created new paths. When you reach certain milestones, it is powerful to connect the dots and consider the emerging story. With any experimentation, whether it is your career or designing a new product or service, you don't start with the full idea, but an overarching sense of what you want to achieve.

This is why we insist on the importance of a north star. A north star and a clear articulation of your values is a powerful combination when making decisions. Throughout the book, we have encouraged you to take on the challenge of examining six aspects of your career. Now, we'd like you to engage in thinking about how you map out the journey. The journey is complicated, although you plan for a relatively straightforward route; in reality, there are multiple stops, a plethora of possibilities, obstacles and opportunities which you cannot envisage upfront. The canvas provides ways for you to decide whether you are facing genuine opportunities or distractions.

Understanding why you do what you do is important, but how often do you think about success and what this means for you? For your career? Many of us only understand purpose and success with hindsight.

It's no surprise that historically the career trajectories for men and women evolve quite differently. Men can set a relatively linear career that experiences minor disruptions. The onslaught of disruption to careers and new technologies inevitably challenges this idea of career trajectories for everyone. Women, however, have negotiated careers with caring responsibilities, as mothers mainly take on the role of primary carer for older and vulnerable family members. In some sectors and regions women still experience institutional biases that exclude them from leadership opportunities. The impact of addressing work and personal responsibilities requires new thinking, primarily because most institutions only had to address inclusivity with a critical mass of female employees. We discussed how women adapted with creative responses in the chapter on creativity. Women's careers, compared to men, are more often described as squiggly or zigzagging. Both of these ideas may be viewed as distractions as they take a different route to achieving leadership goals. Once again, using the sailing analogy, when boats are unable to sail higher than a certain angle towards the wind, they sail 'beating to windward' – in other words, they adopt a zigzag approach to move forward. When facing barriers, finding different approaches creates a way forward, and may get you to your destination faster than taking the planned route.

In this chapter we will explore how you can create your own career trajectory, defining what success looks like to you, how you can craft your roles, adding this touch of creativity to your journey.

Creating your own career trajectory: taking the lead

There was a point when entering the workplace was similar to taking a long drive on an expressway; you knew the end goal and direction and at times your speed varied depending on what or who else was ahead of you. Pretty straightforward. Today, entering the workplace is a completely different situation, with far more nuances and opportunities; not only do you take a variety of routes but also different ways to reach your end goal. Our research shows that tenure in organizations halves every generation. It has gone from 30 years to 15, to seven, and currently stands at a little over three years. The expressway is now shorter, faster, more crowded. And many users are looking at alternative routes: entrepreneurship has never been more popular. It's exciting but it can also be quite daunting and overwhelming.

Susanne Thorning-Lund is a partner in the Board Practice at Odgers Berndtson and specializes in board appointments. She describes the impact of change: 'The transition we have seen in organizations, over the past decade in particular, proactively seeking out and embracing what might before have been labelled "non-traditional" continues at pace. Agility is the key leadership trait – the ability to adapt, adopt and change. The natural trait to partner agility is humility – accepting that you will likely not have all the answers and finding ways to encourage the contribution of differences of thought, perspectives and experience. Success these days hinges as much on the ability of women (and men) to illustrate that what they bring isn't necessarily ever bigger leadership roles, but rather the agility that comes with experience of different industries, roles, ownership structures or whatever it may be. As if we didn't know it, women are ambitious – and they are increasingly vocal and eloquent about their ambitions. They want to be the CEO. They want to be the board chair. Expressing an ambition without badgering is a fine balance, although in some environments and for some roles, badgering could be seen as a positive. But transitioning to the board level means tuning down what could be interpreted as an overly insistent approach.'

At the confluence of the fourth industrial revolution, the post-pandemic normal and the demands for remote and meaningful work from Gen Z, the labour market is undergoing rapid transformation. It is the first time in history that three generations are working simultaneously in organizations. The World Economic Forum (WEF) identifies the following key drivers for change: adoption of new and frontier technologies (AI, big data, the metaverse, bioprinting, quantum computing), increased digital access, integration of ESG (environmental, social and governance) standards, rising cost of living, slower global growth. The list goes on, but if we consider the first issue alone, what will work look like in the future? We are already witnessing occupational transitions as workers need to be reskilled for emerging jobs.

A recent report on generative AI and the future of work in America forecasted the need for an additional 12 million occupational transitions, with workers in lower-wage jobs being 14 times more likely to change occupations. The scale is breathtaking, particularly when you consider the US experienced 8.6 million occupational shifts from 2019 to 2022; clearly the pandemic had a big part to play, speeding up the need to introduce new technologies into jobs.

In another report, the research on countries that represent nearly half of the world's population and over 60 per cent of its GDP shows that 1 in 16 workers may have to switch occupations by 2030. That's over 100 million workers in the following countries: China, France, Germany, India, Japan, Spain, the UK and the US. There are some emerging macro trends that help to make sense of these figures and how you start thinking about your career and the jobs you want to invest in:

- Virtual working will continue but with a balanced hybrid approach.
- E-commerce is continuing to grow at two to five times the pre-pandemic rate, with more diversified applications including telemedicine, online banking and streaming entertainment. The meteoric rise in digital transactions has impacted the growth in associated occupations such as delivery and transport.
- The rise in the adoption of frontier technologies – automation, AI, digital in all its shapes and forms – will both increase the complexity but also encourage leaders to rethink how they assess uncertainty, new approaches to controlling costs, supply change demands, consumer demands, industry dynamics and the like. Data remains the new oil, but knowing how to handle data is as essential and often as confusing as deep-sea drilling or turning crude oil into petroleum.

While change is constant, the current scale of change is quite overwhelming, ripe with both immense opportunities and significant challenges. The current reality makes it even more important that you take charge of your career. For example, if you are currently in the legal industry, data shows that AI will be able to replace the work of over 1,000 lawyers at a time by 2025. And this is an industry that no one could imagine changing in any significant manner. In the US, AI is currently used to determine fines in minor cases of speeding, parking offences, etc. This is only the beginning. So, as a human lawyer, what is your added value? What role do you want to play?

Using diversity to evolve organizational design

Leaders recognize the need to change the nature of their organizations. One way to do that is to engage bright new talent, and a cohort of creative thinkers, in decision-making. Over the last 15 years the focused attention on diversity has created significant momentum in changing the profile of the workforce across management and leadership in most sectors.

Tamara Box, a city lawyer based in London, who has been a fierce advocate for more diversity for decades, recognizes the changes: 'Women professionals in the 1980s and early 1990s were not wired to help each other. So few opportunities were available for a woman to reach a leadership position and every woman felt she had to compete with others of her gender for each slot. And when a woman did get that leadership role, she was possessive about it, wanting to believe that she was unique. She saw no benefit in seeing other women ascend into leadership, because that would remove some of the "special" quality of her accomplishment. Add in years of socialization, whereby children even as young as six years old believe that women are inferior to men, and this is what you get: women fighting each other for the scraps of leadership that fall off men's tables. We are evolving, however. Some women leaders today have learnt that there is power in banding together, supporting each other with a helping hand or word. One of my mantras is: "Lift as you rise." If we all do this, then the rising tide will lift all boats – or all women in this case.'

Deconstructing the barriers

While a great deal of work has been initiated to address barriers and cultures in the workplace, there are still reasons why we are seeing large rates of attrition among women. The third annual *Women @ Work: A global outlook* report from Deloitte showed more women leaving their employer in 2022 than in 2020 and 2021 combined. The reasons why women leave the workplace are complicated and cannot be ascribed to a single factor; however, more work is focusing on how leaders and organizations need to reflect on the cultures that exclude the full participation of women.

The report surveyed 5,000 women across 10 countries and sectors (Australia, Brazil, Canada, China, Germany, India, Japan, South Africa, the UK and the US). Women are still experiencing non-inclusive behaviours and finding it difficult to report these experiences to their employers. Data shows just under half of women surveyed (45 per cent) had experienced microaggressions or harassment in the workplace over the last 12 months. Notably more women are calling out the behaviour, which indicates previous figures underestimated the scale of incidences. In fact, one of the more worrying issues around calling out types of behaviours that make women feel uncomfortable is that the victims feel like the action/words did not feel serious enough to report – this is particularly problematic around microaggressions. Women who have experienced this type of behaviour often do not want to call out these experiences, at the risk of being labelled 'problematic, troublesome, annoying' – everything a good girl is not! Of course, once these labels are assigned it is difficult to get promoted.

Waiting for behaviours to change is an option, but a long-drawn-out one that will only continue to create greater frustration. Each passing generation of women in the workplace is less willing to accept the situation, and is fighting vocally to change it, as was demonstrated by the Me Too movement. While one approach is obviously the design and implementation of norms, regulations, corporate cultures that embrace diversity, it is also essential to understand the barriers – sometimes the fears – that underpin those barriers. And in some cases, identifying allies who will support your diversity agenda, support gender equity and support your leadership career aspirations is an essential individual first step. If this approach seems too piecemeal, then remember people leave because of their immediate environment and women are more likely to leave.

The Lean In McKinsey report, *Women in the Workplace 2022*, surveyed women who had switched jobs in the last two years and identified the following trends. Just under half (48 per cent) moved because of limited opportunities for career advancement, a fifth switched because of an unsupportive manager (22 per cent), restricted flexibility was equally important (20 per cent), followed by 18 per cent leaving because of the organization's lack of commitment to DE&I. Holding an unmanageable workload was the weakest reason why women left (17 per cent).

Take the lead: what will success look like in your career?

The parameters for defining success have become wider and far more interesting. Our women exemplify the impact of different approaches to articulating and demonstrating success. Each one of our women is a role model and each of you is a role model with your connections, perhaps more than you realize. Success is hugely personal, and it would be improper for us to propose a universal model of success. Instead, we are sharing a range of perspectives from our women to inspire and perhaps even challenge some of your assumptions.

The inspiration corner

You have met several impressive and inspiring women across the different chapters of this book. In this inspiration corner, we have asked them how they define success.

Jennifer Publicover: 'I define success in my career as maintaining a growth mindset. Stepping into my current position involved the steepest learning curve I have ever encountered. To be given that experience, at this stage in my career, was a gift. As I become more senior, I reflect on what would have happened if I was not in the room and was not driving this conversation. Would we have had the same outcome? For me, having this impact is important.'

Gwen Billon: 'Professional success is achieving a goal that you set for yourself. I wanted to become a senior member of investment banking, a managing director, a group head – which I achieved in the last few years. But I wanted my professional success married with personal success, and I am happy that I managed my professional endeavours while having a family. One of the reasons I have stayed in banking is because I have always been conscious of who I wanted to work with. Choosing the people who would treat me well, give me interesting projects and opportunities to grow, was a key element. It was not a strategic choice but rather a gut feeling of working for the people that you like.'

Helene Bouyer shared her experiences of living in multiple countries while building a thriving business: 'Success for me was being able to continue my career, adapting to a given environment and context that I had not chosen. I was proud to find a job in countries that were not always easy, while continuing to progress professionally in the same industry.

'This allowed me to keep my own "space", develop my network and work with people from very different origins and backgrounds. Each time it was a very enriching experience that I feel proud of.'

Whitney Gore: 'It is crucial not to confuse personal success with company success – they are two distinct forms of success. I always want the companies I work for to succeed, but I also want my own individual professional success. Success is not linear, and it is not achieving a goal at the end of a long road. Success is measured for me by each role and every stage of my career, and especially by the extent to which I am trusted by my peers to execute and create impact for the business.'

Catherine Clark: 'I define success, frankly, in terms of control. For me, having control over my professional choices, which in turn impact my personal life, is essential to me. So when I started my own company, it was in direct reaction to the fact that I had two choices: I could transition out of my television career and work in the private sector, where I work on someone else's schedule, and for clients who were chosen by my employer, or I could work for myself, choose my clients and choose my hours and have the flexibility to be available to have time with my two small children. And that was the path I took. I think we don't recognize that we have the ability in many cases to make that decision, to establish a little bit more control over our professional lives. Not all women have that choice, obviously, but for me that control element was essential.'

Rumina Velshi: 'My career hallmark is wanting to bring about change. I need to keep an eye on the longer term and what success really looks like. I bear scars in the interim and put up with nonsense but always make sure that the yardstick is moving. It has never been a question of courage but rather of determination and perseverance. Looking back, I have been risk-averse in choosing what I wanted to do. But over time this changed: I wanted to stretch the boundaries. It was during the period when I was playing it safe that I had a realization – I thought to myself, "If you fail, how far can you fall?" It changed my mentality because it brought a greater sense of purpose and self-confidence. If you do not learn to fail, you fail to learn. Taking on risk was not part of the equation early on in my career.

I played it safe. This change in viewpoint was built over time. It was just greater self-confidence and becoming more mature and comfortable in my skin.'

Delphine Inesta: 'Human relations are at the centre of what I consider a successful career. I do not link it to a position or salary, which are usually the objective criteria for defining success. Quite unlikely that power and money are what make you happy at the end of your life. It is about the helpful feeling and the relations you have had during the day, if you were happy at work, and more importantly, if you have been able to be yourself. Life is short! Spending so much time at work not being yourself is a waste of time. Be yourself and everything is going to be fine. You are more powerful when you are yourself. You are happier.'

Human relations are at the centre of what I consider a successful career

Michelle LeSueur: 'What does success mean to me? At a very high level, it's an answer to the questions – Have I made a difference? Am I adding value in my role? In what way am I making an impact to the greater society? I often ask myself how can I leverage my strengths so the people I work with, or those on my team, bring greater science to society to help make a difference for patients? Unfortunately, there are many discrepancies in healthcare and in what medical access is available to patients and that's my motivation. I see, and sit around, people who are incredible scientists, and to be successful would mean propelling their science to patients across the globe. One of my strengths is being a connector and bringing people together. So I want to leverage that in the broadest way I can, not just with my team or within my organization. How can I apply that strength and activate it to attain my goals, so that the impact of incredible science reverberates across the globe?'

Marina: 'For me, a career allows me to have my own identity, a constant through the years, including since having kids. But also, my three children are a great motivator in themselves, to give them the best possible education opportunities in life and setting an example, especially to my daughters. Finally, I am a big believer in financial independence for women and how empowering having it is.'

Naadia Qadr: 'My personal belief is that one should not get too bogged down with the definition of success. Bringing that into the idea of "thinking of oneself as a product" – frequent post-mortems and time-box-based examination of one's journey help assess if the *determine your* initial hypothesis around the definition of *long-term vision* success, i.e. the long-term career goal, was correct. If not, maybe it's time to stop, *for life* breathe and examine the factors that are stymieing your growth.

'Basic tenets of product development that are analogous to our personal life are objective and purpose. It's critical to examine one's purpose, and how – if one were to be a "product" – one could make an impact. Similar to a product, determine your long-term vision for life, then create the strategy and tactics to support and execute on that. Incorporate frequent post-mortems.

'Our journeys, professional or otherwise, are rarely a straight line. There will be many peaks and troughs. However, similar to product development, frequent self-evaluation to assess if you are incrementally progressing towards your goals and objectives prevents disappointment, derailments and failures. Bringing awareness into the everyday decision-making allows you to pivot, or take a lateral path when you hit a road-bump or are stuck.

'In summary, developing and strengthening self-awareness, self-examination, resilience to power through some headwinds, evaluating whether there is incremental progress towards goals are all analogies from the product world that you can apply to yourself.'

> **TAKE THE LEAD!**
>
> Your role models: who are they and what do you admire in them?
>
> What is your own definition of success? Out of the women we have introduced to you, who are you drawn to?
>
> Your role model could be a composite of them. Which part of their definition of success resonated with you?

Crafting your own career using the canvas and your creativity

As you can see in these testimonies from this varied and inspiring group of women, each path is unique, and getting inspired and having role models will help you craft your own career path. Add a piece of creativity in your career journey, by identifying composite role models, redesigning components of your jobs, and learning to pivot.

Let's start with your career – how do you describe your career? When you are thinking about bringing new elements, reformatting your career, what are the elements you need to prioritize?

Identify your composite role models

Crafting your career means you need to take a different approach to how you identify role models. It is highly unlikely that you will find someone who matches your aspirations for your role. Instead, you may find it more useful to identify composite role models, drawing inspiration from a group of people who demonstrate specific skills, behaviours and qualities you admire. The composition of your group of role models creates space for you to flex according to where you are right now, and also widen the influences to include diverse individuals from a range of backgrounds and experiences. Your own role models may not replicate your experiences and perspectives.

Tamara Box: 'I had really interesting role models and I am a big believer in the concept of composite models because nobody is like you. I had amazing and talented role models, both men and women.'

At the same time, it's also important for you to consider, if you haven't already, how you step up as a role model for others. The data on women in careers shows the science, technology, engineering and mathematics (STEM) fields are still struggling with gender parity in leadership functions, and role modelling plays a big part in this puzzle. Building and maintaining the visibility of diverse groups of women in male-dominated fields makes a difference to career aspirations.

There is far more media coverage on women who are breaking the mould, being the first women to achieve status across different fields. The stories of pioneering women in their respective fields are inspirational, but we need to normalize these activities. It is easy to put a woman on a pedestal, but when she is the sole voice, it is also relatively easy to knock down that pedestal. The idea is to build platforms demonstrating the diversity of women in different sectors and regions. This means saying yes to opportunities that are visible and promote you as a role model; when a platform rather than a pedestal is built, it's much harder to topple.

Pivoting or designing – do one or the other.

Job-crafting is an increasingly common and acceptable approach in which organizations and their senior leadership teams are open to individuals redesigning components of a job. Doing this will allow you to create a role that suits you better and is more aligned with your compass. It is not easy to have those discussions, but approaching them from a win-win position, with a clear rationale for why the design is better, is a completely acceptable and understandable conversation.

If you don't have the flexibility yet to redesign your job and you are struggling with motivation and progression, then consider pivoting.

create the change you want, rather than have change happen to you

Pivoting became an important survival tool during the pandemic for organizations and individuals, leaving the field of entrepreneurship and entering that of organizations, individuals and careers. And in a tweak of the famous adage: create the change you want, rather than have change happen to you.

Rhea Aoun-Clavel started as a convertible bond salesperson, then created a start-up, worked in event management and has now requalified as a psychologist – she reflects on how she created the change she wanted: 'I have always considered my career in a fluid and open way, not setting barriers from the start. I never hesitated to change industries every time I felt the need for a change, relentlessly trying to find a job or an industry where I would feel happy and fulfilled. I quickly realized that it was not possible to get there without a good support system, through family and close friends, as well as a larger network of professional contacts. I was amazed and humbled by people's availability and willingness to help me achieve my goal. For years, even though I enjoyed my jobs in the different industries I worked in (finance, technology start-up, event management), I felt that something was missing and that I wasn't entirely fulfilled. Every time I made a career transition, it was because I was in search of more meaning in what I was doing. With time, I increasingly felt the need to make a difference, and to find a job that was aligned with my core values. It took me several years and several career transitions before I found my passion and decided to do a professional reorientation to become a psychologist.'

The canvas sections will help you identify where there are opportunities for change, and what resources you have available to facilitate moving your career forward. Remember what we said earlier: the most effective route isn't always the most straightforward line.

Christine Artero is a full-time arbitrator with the Arbitration Chambers (Singapore) and Fountain Court Chambers (London and Singapore). A dual-qualified lawyer, she is educated in both the civil law and the common law traditions, and she is admitted to the Paris Bar and works as a solicitor in England and Wales. Prior to moving to Singapore, Christine worked in private practice, at Shearman & Sterling and at the London Court of International Arbitration.

Christine explains how she dealt with the change when she moved to Asia in 2013: 'I knew that moving to Singapore could open a lot of opportunities, but it was also taking a leap of faith. I did not know the region and was not familiar with Singapore's arbitration ecosystem. However, I knew that it was vibrant and growing tremendously fast. When I got here, I took a step back to study the market, meet people, assess the work opportunities, and make a plan. At the back of my mind was always the idea of eventually becoming an independent arbitrator, so I decided to explore new roles in the field. I worked as a tribunal secretary to dozens of arbitral tribunals and started to teach arbitration in several reputable institutions, while at the same time familiarizing myself with the APAC region. I received my first appointment as arbitrator two years after setting foot in Asia. My caseload as arbitrator grew over the following three years, and I eventually established myself as a full-time arbitrator in 2018.'

Today, Christine's experience spans a broad range of commercial disputes, and she sits as an arbitrator in cases seated all over the world.

As you review your responses to the different sections in the canvas, you may decide that some things need tweaking, some things will need to radically change, or that you are completely on the course you want to be on, and that an opportunity you were reluctant to take will either take you away from that course or, on the contrary, reinforce the direction you have chosen.

When you are thinking big, do not let your current skill set close doors for you – if you had the skills, if you couldn't fail, what would you do? **Cecile Hillary** shares her perspective on how to handle uncertainty: 'When you move into a job, you need to have 50 per cent of it figured out, and then you need to be able to think that the other 50 per cent you can learn, or you will have people do it for you who are good. I have learnt so much in my current role, especially at the outset, which was incredibly interesting and very exciting. It has really given me almost a new lease in my career – a new boost.'

Delphine Mourot-Haxaire also shares a personal story when she decided to pivot in her career: 'I changed division when I was in banking, and the advice I was given was that I needed to think about this move as a three-leg stool. As long as I was familiar with two legs, I could build on it and learn about the third leg. So, for example, for this move, I knew the product as I was still going to work on fixed-income products, and I knew the person I was going to work with. Thinking about this, what I did not know was the division and moving from the private side to the public side of the bank. I am now often asked about my change from investment banking to higher education. Having made such a big change before, it was a smooth transition because I knew I could adapt and rely on my transferable skills.'

Both **Cecile** and **Delphine** build on their self-efficacy to handle new situations. As we discussed in Chapter 1, transferability of skills is not merely about applying the same techniques in a new environment; it is about using wider emotional skills to become effective in new sectors and organizations. You can't always predict where you will be working, or even the type of work you are doing, but you can have a good idea of how you work and what propels you to work.

Then the question is, really, how do you plan for the how and why? Can you plan this? How are you intentional about this?

It is the balance between recognizing that our life, our longevity and our working style are going to take longer, we have more options available to us, and thinking about your skills as transferable skills.

TAKE THE LEAD!

Take some time to create your job description.

It's up to you to have fun thinking about your role.

What is it that you really do? What is your role that was not included in job description?

What is it about your role that you really enjoy?

Do you have opportunities to keep learning new skills?

Crafting your own career: a creative and entrepreneurial mindset for your career

By now, you have had a chance to think about what success looks like for you, and also identify your role models. You have a blueprint, but how will you execute it? Before you start working on different elements of the canvas, let's take a moment for you to consider how you think about your career. The key element to successful job-crafting is to take a proactive approach to your career, one that is best described as an entrepreneurial mindset.

Deploying an entrepreneurial mindset allows you to rethink what is or is not a true barrier or hurdle and find creative solutions to those barriers. Is it simply that it has not been done before, but is, realistically, possible? Is it unknown but knowable? Is there a way around the barrier? Is the hurdle truly a hurdle or is it perceived as such? And by whom?

The level of complexity at work requires radically different thinking and many of the new roles that will come to be essential in the decades ahead of us do not exist yet, so whether you want to engage in job-crafting or adjust your current role to incorporate frontier technology, most of these positions are yet to be defined. The beauty of this approach is that you can't go wrong. If something does not work for you then you can tweak it; use the squiggly approach to careers to your advantage – as you move sideways, diagonally and upwards, you gain important learning and skills with each experience.

Marianne Desserrieres has worked in the real estate sector as an urbanist and now works in Paris in the cabinet of a minister: 'Now that I am more or less at half of my professional life, I realize it is for me more a "path" than a career. This means that each step was not always conceived as a step towards the following one, but each step by itself was the right moment for me at that time in my life. This could mean acquiring new skills or competences, discovering a new professional environment, using skills developed in the past, transmitting to others, etc. Each new step has been a response to very different needs or motivations. For example, wanting to manage teams did not arise before I had 15 years of professional practice and really mastered a number of skills and competences. It sometimes feels like a challenge to articulate both what I want and the professional opportunities. Is there a good time to spend one year abroad for a long trip, for having children, for taking some time for you or, conversely, deciding to go full steam ahead at work? I have the feeling I am always looking for the exact balance between this professional life, which I want to be stimulating and thrilling, and a personal life which has always been for me the non-negotiable priority.'

Each new step has been a response to very different needs or motivations

Marina, Senior MD in investment banking, current Head of Investors' Relations in a FTSE100, told us that the best advice she ever received was: 'When you get tired, get some rest, don't quit!' She shared with us: 'I have found over the years that women tend to be much more binary with the effort that we put into the job versus the men, feeling that we have to be 100 per cent in all the time or not be in at all.'

Finally, while looking both at the canvas and at your career, and talking about 'some rest', don't forget your energy tank – there is only so much you can do at a certain point, and it is all about prioritizing, and deciding how much of your energy tank you will allocate to each of the Cs we have gone through together.

As we draw together the main elements that nurture your career, let's focus on the top three points we have discussed in this final chapter.

1 Connect the dots – what does success look like to you now? What is your own story?
2 Craft your own career – what are your transferable skills? How can you pivot and grow?
3 Think like an owner – this is your career, so use your creativity, and be intentional and strategic. Where do you put your energy?

TAKE THE LEAD!

Going back to the canvas – how can you draft your dream career, your dream job and how will you get there? Go back to the canvas. It is iterative! What is missing?

Don't forget your energy tank (oxygen tank/reservoir tank/wind in your sails) – which C are you going to prioritize?

- Creativity
- Compass
- Courage
- Connection
- Champions
- Curating teams
- Careers

How will you share your energy among all items of the canvas?

CONCLUSION

Now, as you prepare to set sail, you know where you want to go and why this journey matters. Before you set off you do a check to ensure everything is in place and ready for the journey. So before we let you go, we are sharing a few thoughts.

What's luck got to do with it?

Whatever the reason for you to pick up this book, you are now at a point where you better understand what you need for your leadership, and how important it is to plan and develop the resources you require. When we started developing the idea for this book, we wanted to write about how women perceive their careers and how much of their success they attribute to luck. By luck we mean good fortune, fate – events outside our control that provide opportunities for us. After many conversations over many months, we recognized luck comes in different forms and has many meanings depending on cultural contexts and learnt behaviours, and even the intersection of faith. We decided to demonstrate how it manifests for different women, but also to highlight how you have a great deal of influence in how you shape and achieve your career aspirations.

Among the women we surveyed, we noticed some interesting trends around luck and leadership behaviours. Women demonstrated a strong relationship between luck and comfort with agile thinking – switching into different thinking modes. More interestingly, when you break down the data by region it is not statistically relevant, which means the drivers for luck are not culturally bound.

However, the level of seniority was far more impactful, with women in C-suite roles acknowledging the impact of luck on their career success. We can see that perceptions around luck are common for women irrespective of their cultural background. The position on luck opens a wider discussion that we often encounter in global programmes. Women face similar barriers to their leadership advancement, irrespective of where they are located. What matters is how women access resources to navigate these barriers for their careers. The women we interviewed have stories to tell that are inspiring to us and they come from very different countries and sectors, and yet their experience coalesced around their perspectives on their leadership and how they navigated through challenges. We have created a chorus of voices from our women sharing their perspectives on luck and how it has impacted their careers.

Helene Bouyer: 'I was lucky, as I was given the chance to succeed. Luck is something that you must build and put all the chips on your side, then luck can arrive. Luck is not by being passive, but rather being active and working like hell.

'You must set career goals as soon as you enter working life, and try to stick to them, whatever the context. For me, this is the only way to build your career.'

Dominique: 'Fortune favours those who are prepared. You can train to have a positive mindset and be open to opportunities that arise, probably randomly. I am curious and interested in lots of things. This has opened numerous doors and reflected later in my career, interestingly.'

Caroline Flanagan: 'I attribute some of my success to luck. I've worked really hard to get where I am, this I know for sure. But without doubt, luck has played a role in that. I was lucky to be sent to the school I went to. Lucky to have people believe in me and tell me I had the potential. But I don't use this against myself. One of the powerful thoughts I have about myself is "I create my own luck." This allows me to recognize luck as a factor without downplaying the hard work and determination it took to get here or needing to be lucky in the future in order to keep progressing.'

Rumina Velshi: 'Luck is when you have an intersection of opportunities and preparedness. You are in charge of bringing luck to yourself because opportunities may be there, you may not even be aware of them or you're not ready to seize them. Luck played a huge part in my life, because I was being aware of how things were evolving around me and was in the right place at the right time. I advise my mentees: you need to take charge of your career. Opportunities will be out there – knocking on your door or floating around. You need to be aware to seize them.'

Cecile Hillary: 'I find it extraordinary when people, particularly people in the Western countries, don't recognize the importance of luck. I mean, after all, the biggest luck is obviously having been born, where I was born, the time I was born and the family that I was born in. I wasn't born into a wealthy family, but I had opportunities in terms of education. My family had the means intellectually, culturally, financially to get me an education and to effectively make sure that money was not an issue or an obstacle. Health is also a part of this in different ways. Honestly, I think luck is something that is undeniable. I think it has to influence the way we think ourselves about opening doors, about diversity and social mobility, which has previously been very rigid.'

Delphine Inesta: 'We are educated to think that we should leave as little as possible to luck and that we should try to control our lives as much as possible. Nevertheless, this is not possible, and I would say that luck has had an important role in my career, specifically in meeting people. Luck is at the centre of a lot of things and if you meet the right people who are going to motivate you or who are going to trust you to have more power and bigger roles, then you are launched to a new step in your career. As far as my career is concerned, I was lucky enough to meet the right people who have been able to show me what I could do and to what extent I could develop. You have to seize the opportunity that unfolds from that starting point. You have to think reversely and try to eliminate the impact of bad luck. Luck is one thing. But what you can build on it is another.'

Marie Planckaert: 'We need to acknowledge that there is an element of luck in success. We do not always realize that both choices and luck are important and often linked. It can happen that you "create" your luck through the choices made. I am convinced that there are tons of people who are very talented, more talented than I am. I made some bold choices and had a bit of luck in having the right people around me at the right time. There are numerous consequences of the choices you made in your career, or your life. I like to look back at those choices with sympathy to the past "me" who made some of the choices without really knowing how everything would unfold. And thankfully we cannot encompass every scenario our choices unfold, because otherwise you would never make any.'

Whitney Gore: 'Luck is a factor of being able to identify the opportunity and convert it to results. I have had a lot of opportunities present themselves because I am willing to take risks. Hence, I have had a lot of luck in my career. But I have taken a lot of risks in seizing those opportunities and pursuing them.'

Gwen Billon: 'You have to create your own luck. It is about anticipating what might happen, to be well-positioned for it and seize a rising opportunity thanks to experience or motivation. If you leave everything to luck, then you could leave your own fate in other people's hands outside your control, and you do not necessarily know if they value what is right for you.'

Catherine Clark: 'I would say luck has played a huge role in my career. And I find this a very interesting question because I think we tend to pretend that luck doesn't necessarily have anything to do with our lives and I feel very much that luck is a huge component. It doesn't mean that we don't work hard. It doesn't mean that we don't have goals or that we don't establish a path we try to follow. But there is absolutely no question that circumstances can sometimes work in our favour and sometimes work against us. And so I would say that I've been very lucky in my career, but there have also been situations I have been able to capitalize on unexpectedly, which have helped me evolve professionally too. So I would say that we all need to accept that luck is a valuable part of our personal and professional journeys. And we need to seize opportunities when they come along. Because some of those opportunities are frankly just pure blind luck.'

Sheikha Alanoud Al Thani emphasizes that: 'Success is not a matter of luck alone. Achieving recognition and awards requires active involvement, meaningful engagements and meticulous reputation-building efforts. While luck plays a role, timing and proactive endeavours are paramount. Merely hoping for success without taking active steps, such as participating in meetings and enhancing one's reputation, will not lead to becoming the next CEO. Success is a result of deliberate actions and strategic decisions.'

Michelle LeSueur: 'Luck: preparation meets opportunity. I would not say my career is just luck. I always wanted to work internationally. It was just a matter of being ready and having that right opportunity. It did not happen overnight. It was the preparation and thinking about what the next opportunity could be like, and then the opening became available.'

Karen Woodham: 'There is no quick way or overnight success! No luck involved – hard bloody work! It is a combination of having a purpose or goal, the determination, discipline and consistency to make it happen, mixed with ability to be creative on how you get there, e.g. taking side moves and re-evaluating as you go! Checking in with yourself every so often and having the courage to change direction or goal!'

Cecilia Weckstrom: 'We think we're lucky because we tend to be humbler, but what we don't realize is, the way we work and do things, we typically create our own luck by forging connections – combining different things and trying various stuff out.

Basically, you're throwing a lot of seeds in the ground, and guess what, some stuff is just going to grow from that. And by magic, you're going to have a fantastic plant one day and that is luck, which has been seeded or cultivated. You see it in that luck by having some of these behaviours.'

Tamara Box: 'There's no question that luck plays a big part in our careers, but I've always believed that the harder I work the luckier I get. Having said that, some aspects of luck are simply luck: I was fortunate to be born into a family that valued education and respected my choices about where and what to study, such as when I gave up a substantial academic scholarship at a Texas university to move to London to study at the London School of Economics. We have no control over where we're born, who our parents are, or how financial circumstances may affect our childhoods. But we can increase our luck if we seize the opportunities that present themselves – call it right place, right time. Then work hard to get even luckier!'

Nadia Verjee: 'I was in London, my parents lived in Dubai. I was travelling to see my mom every three months. It was 2008, I was looking to do something different. I went out for lunch with a friend who introduced me to their friend. I mentioned I was working in politics. He said, "I'm working on the design of the International Affairs Office of the Prime Minister. Send me your CV and I'll send it along." By the next month, I was working as the European Desk Officer in that office. Where does that conversation and outcome happen? Yeah, so it's serendipity. Maybe there's a degree of serendipity, but can I add to it 100 per cent? Have I done everything since to earn everything I've ever done? I have, 1,000 per cent.'

M B Christie: 'I've often said, be prepared to be lucky. Luck has been essential to the twists and turns my career has taken. The fall of the Berlin Wall brought me to Europe from the US as a foreign correspondent 33 years ago, and I haven't left. Failure to sell my business in Prague brought me to London just as the first dot-com boom was sweeping us all into the digital age. That

led to a 25-plus-year career in the new discipline of digital product management. Over the years, I've taken some big leaps at
different junctures, and I've always landed on my feet due to
luck and stubbornness. Women are half the world's population
and the only ones responsible for bearing the next generation of
our species. We should be partners, not diversity statistics. I'm
frustrated that we women are now invited to the dance, but we
still aren't dancing in the corporate powerhouses of the world.
We are naturals at the skills needed in the digital age – collaboration, listening, empathy, patience, change management (who
primarily manages the children as they change from year to
year?), coupled with an urgency to get stuff done. As a non-
executive director, I see our skills shine in the boardrooms, but I
know these same women have been overlooked around executive tables.'

Virginie Melin: 'How much do I attribute luck to success?
Well, luck and no luck also! Most probably success is when,
despite no luck, there is still success, learning and growth, and
still love. I don't feel I got things by luck professionally. But I was
lucky to meet and work for people who trusted me and helped
me grow, and for that I feel very lucky.'

Lamice Hourani: 'Nothing happens by chance. For me, luck
has nothing to do with it. It's all about faith. We become what
we believe.'

Marina: 'I believe one makes one's own luck most of the time.
I'd say that I don't rely on it but, for sure, take advantage of it.
Serendipity is a thing!'

Emeline Chapelon: 'I am a paediatrician doctor in a hospital.
For a long time, I thought it was always the same doctors who
had difficult night shifts with serious and stressful cases during
their shifts, lots of people randomly arriving at the same time,
and too many things to manage during the night... like being a
"black cat" at night, a symbol of misfortune. I thought I was
fortunate not to be a "black cat". But after a while, I told myself
that it wasn't just luck that gave me less stressful night shifts but

probably my way of seeing things, anticipating and managing them.'

Rhea Aoun-Clavel: 'When I first started working, I believed that all the positive evolutions in my career were due to pure luck. Reflecting on this 20 years later, I believe that the determination and relentless efforts I put into my different career transitions paid off. Connecting with as many people as possible in the industries I was interested in multiplied several-fold the chance encounters and interesting opportunities.'

The perspectives on luck are as varied as the women and a strong reminder there is no one way to achieve success. Throughout the book we have used the analogy of a boat because your career is about progress and allowing you to decide how you navigate a route – there is no road map, just milestones to guide you.

As we were writing the book, we started to identify many other Cs: for example, Curiosity – a significant attribute for creativity, as one does not exist without the other. Caring – self-care, protecting your health and wellbeing, building your resilience. Consistency – we are dazzled by shooting stars, but we really need strong performers who are regular and reliable. Celebration – our softest C, but one that deserves special attention now. Taking time, regularly, to celebrate is as important as any of the other Cs in this book. This is not specifically about self-care or building resilience, although it makes a huge difference, but it is about celebrating you, your success and your achievements. When leadership is so tightly aligned with a strong sense of purpose, we can forget to step back and validate ourselves, or, being our own harshest critics, we see what we didn't do and forget the phenomenal impact of work. So if we may, we add this C and encourage you to build in moments of celebration.

This isn't really the end but the start of what we expect to be a journey filled with excitement, challenges and immense joy. Taking the helm as a leader requires responsibility and all the elements we discuss in the canvas, but there are moments of pure joy, when you connect with colleagues and are a part of their success, when projects that were deemed impossible come to fruition, when you step back and realize how far you have come in your journey.

Bon voyage and bon courage. And remember – opportunities and luck are yours for the taking.

REFERENCES

Introduction

World Economic Forum (2020) *Global Gender Gap*, www.weforum.org/reports/gender-gap-2020-report-100-years-pay-equality/ (archived at https://perma.cc/4HSR-95UJ)

World Economic Forum (2023) *Global Gender Gap*, www.weforum.org/reports/global-gender-gap-report-2023/ (archived at https://perma.cc/T684-BUKL)

Chapter 1: Creativity

Amabile, T (1998) How to kill creativity, *Harvard Business Review*, September–October

Helzer, E and Kim, S (2019) Creativity for workplace well-being, *Academy of Management Perspectives*, 33 (2), doi.org/10.5465/amp.2016.0141 (archived at https://perma.cc/GWY9-USBA)

Hoomans, J (2015) 35,000 decisions: The great choices of strategic leaders, Leadingedge, go.roberts.edu/leadingedge/the-great-choices-of-strategic-leaders (archived at https://perma.cc/M7PJ-2JCS)

Kahneman, D (2011) *Thinking, Fast and Slow*, 8th ed, Farrar, Straus and Giroux

Kahneman, D and Amos, T (1979) Prospect theory: An analysis of decision under risk, *Econometrica*, 47 (2), 263–91

Mueller, J, Melwani, S and Goncalo, J (2011) The bias against creativity: Why people desire but reject creative ideas, *Psychological Science*, 23, 13–7, 10.1177/0956797611421018

Ogden, L E (2019) Working mothers face a 'wall' of bias – but there are ways to push back, *Science*, 10 April, www.science.org/content/article/working-mothers-face-wall-bias-there-are-ways-push-back (archived at https://perma.cc/N647-EBNF)

Proudfoot, D, Kay, A and Koval, C Z (2015) A gender bias in the attribution of creativity: Archival and experimental evidence for the perceived association between masculinity and creative thinking, *Psychological Science*, 26, 10.1177/0956797615598739

Samuelson, W and Zeckhauser, R (1988) Status quo bias in decision making, *Journal of Risk and Uncertainty*, Springer, 1 (1), 7–59

Schafler, K M (2023) *The Perfectionist's Guide to Losing Control: A path to peace and power*, Portfolio

Schwab, K (2017) *Fourth Industrial Revolution*, World Economic Forum

Shen, H (2018) Does the adult brain really grow new neurons?, *Scientific American*, 7 March, www.scientificamerican.com/article/does-the-adult-brain-really-grow-new-neurons/ (archived at https://perma.cc/JCL7-PUE9)

Verniers, C and Vala, J (2018) Justifying gender discrimination in the workplace: The mediating role of motherhood myths, *PLOS ONE*, 13 (7), doi.org/10.1371/journal.pone.0201150 (archived at https://perma.cc/EAC3-NGLY)

Chapter 2: Compass

Gallup Workplace Survey (2023) Why trust in leaders is faltering and how to gain it back, 17 April, www.gallup.com/workplace/473738/why-trust-leaders-faltering-gain-back.aspx (archived at https://perma.cc/93FG-T98M)

Haden, J (2019) Steve Jobs said 1 thing separates successful people from everyone else (and will make all the difference in your life), Inc blog, www.inc.com/jeff-haden/steve-jobs-said-1-thing-separates-successful-people-from-everyone-else-and-will-make-all-difference-in-your-life.html (archived at https://perma.cc/LRU3-ATUT)

Horovitz, J and Ohlsson-Corboz, A-V (2007) *A Dream with a Deadline: Turning strategy into action*, Financial Times/Prentice Hall, London

World Economic Forum Report (2023) Why strong company values are essential for attracting the next generation of professionals, www.weforum.org/agenda/2023/04/why-company-values-deal-breaker-next-generation-professionals/ (archived at https://perma.cc/MAV2-LRY9)

Chapter 3: Courage

Al-Qahtani, A M, Ibrahim, H A, Elgzar, W T, El Sayed, H A and Essa, R M (2021) The role of self-esteem and self-efficacy in women empowerment in the Kingdom of Saudi Arabia: A cross-sectional study, *African Journal of Reproductive Health*, 25 (1), 69–78

Babcock, L, Peyser, B, Vesterlund, L and Weingart L (2020) *The No Club: Putting a stop to women's dead-end work*, Piatkus

Bandura, A (1978) Reflections on self-efficacy, *Advances in Behaviour Research and Therapy*, 1 (4), 237–69, doi.org/10.1016/0146-6402(78)90012-7 (archived at https://perma.cc/4UCW-RFX8)

Bennett, J (2017) *Feminist Fight Club: An office survival manual for a sexist workplace*, Harper Wave

Brown, B (2012) *Daring Greatly: How the courage to be vulnerable transforms the way we live, love, parent and lead*, Gotham Books

Bruckmüller, S and Branscombe N R (2011) How women end up on the 'glass cliff', *Harvard Business Review*, January-February, hbr.org/2011/01/how-women-end-up-on-the-glass-cliff (archived at https://perma.cc/69T6-NZWE)

Glass, C and Cook, A (2020) Pathways to the glass cliff: A risk tax for women and minority leaders?, *Social Problems*, 67 (4), 637–53

Hartman, R L and Barber, E G (2020) Women in the workforce: The effect of gender on occupational self-efficacy, work engagement and career aspirations, *Gender in Management*, 35 (1), 92–118

Janjuha-Jivraj, S (2023) The tyranny of politeness limits your career prospects, *Forbes*, www.forbes.com/sites/shaheenajanjuhajivrajeurope/2023/07/06/the-tyranny-of-politeness-limits-your-career-prospects/ (archived at https://perma.cc/Q8AN-UWN2)

Jeffers, S (2007) *Feel the Fear and Do It Anyway*, Vermilion.

Molinksi, A (2017) *Reach: A new strategy to help you step outside your comfort zone, rise to the challenge and build confidence*, Avery

Morgenroth, A T, Kirby, T A, Ryan, M K, and Sudkämper, A (2020) The who, when, and why of the glass cliff phenomenon: A meta-analysis of appointments to precarious leadership positions, *Psychological Bulletin*, 146 (9), 797

O'Brien, K R (2014) Just saying no: An examination of gender differences in the ability to decline requests in the workplace, Rice University

Obama, M (2018) *Becoming*, Random House

Singh, S K, Pradhan, R K, Panigrahy, N P and Jena, L K (2019) Self-efficacy and workplace well-being: Moderating role of sustainability practices, *Benchmarking*, 26 (6), 1692–708

Swart, T, Chisholm, K and Brown, P (2015) *Neuroscience for Leadership: Harnessing the brain gain advantage*, Palgrave Macmillan

Chapter 4: Connections

Araújo-Pinzón, P, Álvarez-Dardet, C, Ramón-Jerónimo, J M and Flórez-López, R (2017) Women and inter-organizational boundary spanning: A way into upper management? *European Research on Management and Business Economics*, 23 (2), 70–81, doi.org/10.1016/j.iedeen.2016.11.001 (archived at https://perma.cc/MY5G-RRQH)

Friedman, R A and Podolny, J (1992) Differentiation of boundary spanning roles: Labor negotiations and implications for role conflict, *Administrative Science Quarterly*, 37 (1), 28–47, doi.org/10.2307/2393532 (archived at https://perma.cc/TQU3-UY7H)

Gladwell, M (2002) *The Tipping Point: How little thanks can make a big difference*, Back Bay Books

Greguletz, E, Diehl, M-R and Kreutzer, K (2019) Why women build less effective networks than men: The role of structural exclusion and personal hesitation, *Human Relations*, 72 (7), 1234–61, doi.org/10.1177/0018726718804303 (archived at https://perma.cc/AV2L-83UY)

Hochschild, A R and Machung A (2021) *The Second Shift: Working parents and the revolution at home*, 3rd edn, Viking Penguin

Janjuha-Jivraj, S (2003) The sustainability of social capital within ethnic networks, *Journal of Business Ethics*, 47, 31–43

Lazarsfeld, P and Merton, R K (1954) Friendship as a social process: A substantive and methodological analysis. In: Berger, M, Abel, T and Charles, H, eds, *Freedom and Control in Modern Society*, Van Nostrand.

Read, S, Sarasvathy, S, Dew, N, Wiltbank, R and Ohlsson, A-V (2010) *Effective Entrepreneurship*, Routledge, London.

Reisinger, D (2010) Sorry, Facebook friends: Our brains can't keep up, CNET, 25 January, CNET, www.cnet.com/home/smart-home/sorry-facebook-friends-our-brains-cant-keep-up/ (archived at https://perma.cc/XGN7-VDQH)

UN (2023) SDG Summit and #UNGA78 High-Level Week Preview: Amina J Mohammed and Special Guests, www.youtube.com/watch?v=C3Gihrs7vRs (archived at https://perma.cc/26U4-9GPS)

Zhang, E, Aven, B and Kleinbaum, A M (2022) Left but not forgotten: Gender differences in networks and performance following mobility, SSRN 3692599 (unpublished)

Chapter 5: Championing

coachingfederation.org (archived at https://perma.cc/6W6F-FP9F)

EMCC Global, Mentoring, www.emccglobal.org/leadership-development/leadership-development-mentoring/#:~:text=EMCC%20Definition%20of%20Mentoring,experience%20sharing%2C%20and%20role%20modelling (archived at https://perma.cc/KV78-5V2S)

Graham, C (2019) Literature review: The gap between mentoring theory and practice for diverse women faculty, *Mentoring and Tutoring: Partnership in Learning*, 27 (2), 131–43

Greguletz, E, Diehl, M R and Kreutzer, K (2019) Why women build less effective networks than men: The role of structural exclusion and personal hesitation, *Human Relations*, 72 (7), 1234–61

Ibarra, H (2019) A lack of sponsorship is keeping women from advancing into leadership, *Harvard Business Review*, 19 August

Janjuha-Jivraj, S (2018) If you think Cinderella only exists in fairytales, look around your office, *Forbes*, 24 October, www.forbes.com/sites/shaheenajanjuhajivrajeurope/2018/10/24/if-you-think-cinderella-only-exists-in-fairy-tales-look-around-your-office/ (archived at https://perma.cc/6KPW-Q6YK)

Janjuha-Jivraj, S and Chisholm, K (2016) *Championing Women Leaders: Beyond sponsorship*, Palgrave Macmillan

Johnson, W B and Smith, D G (2018) How men can become better allies to women, *Harvard Business Review*, 11, 10–15

Chapter 6: Curating your team

Eagly, A and Johannesen-Schmidt, M (2001) The leadership styles of women and men, *Journal of Social Issues*, 54 (4), 781–97

Herrando, C and Constantinider, E (2021) Emotional contagion: A brief overview and future directions, *Frontiers Psychology*, 12, doi.org/10.3389/fpsyg.2021.712606 (archived at https://perma.cc/FD5B-WU2M)

Chapter 7: Career

Deloitte (2023) *Women @ Work 2023: A global outlook*, www2.deloitte.com/content/dam/Deloitte/si/Documents/deloitte-women-at-work-2023-a-global-outlook.pdf (archived at https://perma.cc/YZ55-XS68)

McKinsey (2022) Women in the Workplace, www.mckinsey.com/~/media/mckinsey/featured%20insights/diversity%20and%20inclusion/women%20in%20the%20workplace%202022/women-in-the-workplace-2022.pdf (archived at https://perma.cc/34FR-59EC)

McKinsey (2023) Generative AI and the future of work in America, www.mckinsey.com/mgi/our-research/generative-ai-and-the-future-of-work-in-america (archived at https://perma.cc/3J9W-K2WD)

McKinsey (2023) What is the future of work?, www.mckinsey.com/featured-insights/mckinsey-explainers/what-is-the-future-of-work (archived at https://perma.cc/AX3G-HK86)

ACKNOWLEDGEMENTS

As academics, researchers and practitioners, we are constantly asking 'Why?', questioning our way into new thoughts, theories, ideas, and testing these against practice, in the real world. Writing a book is one way of making sense of the wealth of content, one way of structuring findings into a meaningful framework.

This book started as a labour of passion, determination and, yes, love. We connected through a common desire to bring a different approach to capability-building for women in leadership roles, with one purpose: support each individual in their journey, celebrating creativity, problem-solving, innovative thinking, drive, determination, strength, success.

The starting point of this project was a series of women's leadership programmes delivered in Europe and the Middle East, providing different vantage points to allow women to understand how to develop their leadership from their unique strengths. These in turn led us to reflect on similarities and differences across the cohorts. The need to answer specific questions, coupled with our research, led to the book you are now holding.

We talk about book writing but, in reality, we have been creating a new approach to leadership that plays to the strengths of women. Creativity is core to this book and has been a significant element in how we think about what women bring to the table.

One of the most rewarding aspects of our work is meeting amazing individuals, who bring a strong sense of commitment and purpose to their leadership. Our gratitude goes to our women contributors: Sheikha Alanoud Al Thani, Aminata Kane, Anna Abulhoul, Benedicte de Gelder, Caroline Flanagan, Catherine Clark, Cecile Hillary, Cecilia Weckstrom, Christine

Artero, Claudia Parzani, Delphine Inesta, Eleri J Dixon, Elise Badoy, Emeline Chapelon, Florence Westemann, Gwen Billon, Jennifer Publicover, Joy Mpofu, Karen Woodham, Kathy Michaels, Lady (Kitty) Chisholm, Kshama Pardhan, Lamice Hourani, Lauren Onthank, Lucie-Claire Vincent, Marianne Desserrieres, Marie Planckaert, Marina Shchuckina, M B Christie, Michele Oliver, Michelle LeSueur, Motunrayo Olagun, Naadia Qadr, Nadia Verjee, Rhea Aoun, Rumina Velshi, Sarah de Lagarde, Susanne Thorning-Lund, Tamara Box, Thoraya Obaid, Virginie Melin, Whitney Gore, Yolanda Azanza. We hope we have done justice to your experiences.

As always, this type of project comes with an army of supporters who provide introductions and additional conversations to further shape our thinking. Thank you to everyone who supported our survey, distributing it to their connections and fantastic individuals who connected us to women for interviews or provided feedback: Britta Pfister, Folly Bah Thibault, Gachoucha Kretz, Krishna Santhanam, Laetitia Paeme, Dr Marcelle Laliberte, Patti Brown, Sebastien Mourot, Stephane Dubois. Thank you to our project team: Haider Ahmar, Vanessa Kolovos, Christopher Ohlsson, Thandiwe Mkhetshane, Amerilda Dyrma and Taiyyaba Kazim – for her creative input on the canvas.

Thank you to our editors Matt James and Susi Lowndes at Kogan Page, as well as Jane Woodhead, for their enthusiasm, their trust and their immense support.

From Anne-Valérie: To my sons, Christopher and Alexander, who inspire me, help me grow and are part of that generation of young men who will, really, change the world. To my partner, Alain-Philippe, whose leadership style, emotional intelligence and humility are a source of inspiration.

From Shaheena: For my boys, Iliyan, Kais and Zayn – whose curiosity and humour constantly keep me on my toes and pushing us further for new adventures. To Zahir, for 25 years of immense patience, love and humour.

From Delphine: To my husband, Sebastien, for his unwavering support and boundless encouragement. To my boys, Arthur and Louis, who are my constant source of strength and energy, and the driving force that compels me to push the boundaries.

From all of us: To our families and our tribes of girlfriends, we are so grateful you are in our lives – thank you.

INDEX

The index is filed in alphabetical, word-by-word order. Numbers in main headings are filed as spelt out in full; acronyms are filed as presented. Page locators in *italics* denote information contained within a Table.

adaptation 7, 18, 23, 24, 45–47, 173,
    180, 186, 194
adaptive perfectionism 41
advertising 26–27, 62, 63, 64
advocacy 81, 137, 140, 144, 145
    see also champions; sponsorship
affective versus cognitive conflict
    163–64
Africa Business Forum 118
agility 34, 39–40, 55, 82, 124, 154,
    173, 181, 199
AI 182, 183
Aidha 110
Al Thani, Sheikha Alanoud 90,
    104–05, 117–18, 140, 203
Amos, Tversky 24
Anne-Valérie (Corboz, Anne-Valérie)
    5, 32, 51
Aoun-Clavel, Rhea 192, 206
Arbitration Chambers 193
Artero, Christine 193
assertiveness 77, 85, 86, 89, 90, 155
attrition 2, 184–85
    see also employment tenure
authoritarian leadership 153
authoritative leadership 153
autonomy 95–96, 161

balcony approach 48
Bandura, Albert 98
Barber, Emily 98
belonging 57, 67, 68, 167
bias 23, 24, 26, 158
    gender 29–30, 89, 99
    institutional 3, 6, 179
    maternal wall 35
Billon, Gwen 36, 74, 104, 114, 135,
    154–55, 186, 202
board development 73–74, 109,
    162–63, 180–81, 205

body language 92
boundary management 72, 77, 87, 120
boundary spanning 119, 120–21, 126
Bouyer, Helene 33–34, 158–59, 186,
    200
Box, Tamara 54–55, 88, 91, 162,
    183–84, 191, 204
boys' networks 137
BP 142, 160
brain function 90, 119
    see also dopamine
brain plasticity 22, 44–45, 93
brand building 142–44, 146, 147
Branscombe, Nyla 101
brokerage 115–16, 120
Brown, Brene 74–75, 76
Bruckmuller, Susanne 101
buddies 48
bullying 87
burnout 40, 72, 86, 99, 170

Canadian Nuclear Safety Commission
    (CNSC) 78–79, 149, 172
canvas framework 12–13, *15*, 136,
    177–78, 179, 190–95, 198
career progression (promotions)
    75–76, 87–88, 98–99,
    136–37, 154, 177–98
    see also champions; coaching; glass
        cliff positions; mentors;
        stretch roles
career success 99–100, 178–81,
    185–90, 203
Cecile (Hillary, Cecile) 37–38, 52, 59,
    76, 94, 127–28, 148–49,
    194, 201
challenging skills 162–63, 167
Chambers of Commerce 111
champion profile 133, 137, 139–40,
    144–45

champions 131–50
    see also advocacy; sponsorship
change 32–37, 48, 56, 181, 182–83
change agency 31–32, 155–56,
    187–88
Chapelon, Emeline 205–06
check-ins 117, 122, 169
Chisholm, Kitty 90, 132
Christian Dior 62
Christie, M. B. 144, 204–05
Christie's 67
Cinderella syndrome 136–37, 142
Claire 128–29
Clark, Catherine 89–90, 156, 187,
    202–03
CNSC 78–79, 149, 172
co-creation 67, 147
coaching 8, 100, 115, 133–34, 149,
    169
codes of conduct 58
cognitive versus affective conflict
    163–64
collaboration 19–20, 80, 120, 124,
    156, 205
communication skills 34, 120
    see also body language; dialogue;
        listening skills; negotiation
        skills; question techniques
compass framework 49–69
compasses 49
complexity 20–22, 196
compound networking 123–24
compromise 56, 60, 63, 88
Conference on Sustainable
    Development (UN) 25
conferences 110, 128
conflict 65–66, 72–74, 163–66
    see also dissent
conflict zone leadership 103–05
connections 107–30
    see also networking
connector status 126–27, 188
continuous improvement 20, 31–32
control 11, 61, 187
    see also emotional regulation
control structures 10–11
conviction 54–55, 71–72, 85–92
Corboz, Anne-Valérie 5, 32, 51
core skills 34

corporate social responsibility (CSR)
    26, 54, 61
courage 42–43, 52–53, 65–67,
    71–105, 159
Covid-19 pandemic 8, 33, 60, 61, 64,
    72, 127, 171–72, 182, 192
creative buddies 48
creativity 8, 17–48, 66, 73, 91, 92–105,
    128–29, 154, 167–69
creativity aversion 23
crisis management 43–44
cross-functional teams 79, 171
cultural norms 33, 63–64, 89, 90,
    129–30, 159
    organizational 24–25, 30–31,
        37–38, 58, 60–61, 134, 140
Curie, Marie 51
curiosity 18–19, 23–24, 39–40, 47,
    81, 128, 144–45, 159, 160

data 182
DE&I 12, 54, 147–48, 185
    see also diversity; inclusion
deadlines 51, 86, 170
decision-making 20–22, 43, 75, 84
delegative leadership 153, 161
delivery 80–81, 85–86, 99, 112, 162
democratic leadership 153
Desserrieres, Marianne 196
developing countries 25, 103–05
dialogue 47, 53, 166–67
directness 78
disabilities 46, 63–64
dissent 30–31
    see also conflict
diversity 7–8
career progression 183–84
    and champions 135–36, 137–38,
        148–49
    and connections 129
    and courage 73–74, 79
    and creativity 27, 37–38, 45
    team building 160, 162–64
Dixon, Eleri J. (Eleri) 79–80, 141,
    166–67
domestic (personal) responsibilities
    113–14, 179–80
Dominique 88, 94, 99, 122–23,
    123–24, 200

dopamine 38–39
Dream with a Deadline (Corboz & Horowitz) 51
drive (grit) 9, 154, 156
Dunbar, Professor Robin 119

e-commerce 182
Eleri (Dixon, Eleri J.) 79–80, 141, 166–67
emotional contagion 170
emotional intelligence 152, 154
emotional regulation 90, 154, 170
empathy 53, 78, 136, 142, 155–56, 157–58, 163, 205
employee resource groups 115
employment tenure 180
  see also attrition
Endurance (ship) 10
endurance (trait) 43
entrepreneurial mindset 12, 108, 113, 124, 180, 195–97
entry-level job applications 62
equitable leadership 170–71
ESG 58, 181
ethics 49–50, 51, 52, 53, 57–62, 65, 66, 68
experimentation (testing) 66, 78, 79, 103, 168, 179
exploration 11, 21–22, 32
Expo City Dubai 85–86

facial expressions 170
failure (mistakes) 13, 79–82, 93–95, 102–03, 104–05, 187–88
'farming for dissent' 30–31
fault lines 164
fear 75–76
feedback 30, 48, 55, 79, 129, 140, 146
Feminist Fight Club (Bennett) 96–97
field-focused leadership 157
fixed mindset 39
Flanagan, Caroline 100, 200–01
flat organizational structures 167
flexibility 10, 11, 38, 62, 95–96, 171–72, 185, 187
flexible stress response 22
Flutter 137–38
Fountain Court Chambers 193

Gen X 57
Gen Z 57, 58, 181
gender 161–63
gender bias 29–30, 89, 99
  see also institutional bias
gender parity 2, 27, 191
gendered modesty 116
General Assembly 25
generative AI 182
glass cliff positions 100–03
global financial crisis (2008-2009) 58
global teams 163–67
goal setting 200, 203
  see also objective setting
Goleman, Daniel 154
Gore, Whitney (Whitney) 30–31, 31–32, 95, 122, 125, 168, 187, 202
grit 9, 154, 156
growth mindset 47, 95, 186

harassment 60, 87, 172, 184
hard power 174
Hartman, Rosanne 98
HEC 5, 28
Helzer, Eric 22
heroism 63, 75
hierarchical organizational structures 10–11, 135, *153*, 167, 174
Hillary, Cecile (Cecile) 37–38, 52, 59, 76, 94, 127–28, 148–49, 194, 201
hippocampus 22
hiring 30, 37, 159–60, 166
homophily 114–15, 120, 135, 136, 174
Honest Talk 89
horizontal (lateral) organizational structures 11, 171
Horovitz, Jacques 51
Hourani, Lamice 95–96, 205
human capital development 57
human relations (relationships) 104, 188
humility 76, 95, 173, 181
hybrid working 127–28, 169, 171, 172, 182
  see also remote (virtual) working
identity 188

impact 52, 53, 67, 143
imposter syndrome 4, 5, 96–100, 102, 104, 140, 175
in-person conferences 128
inclusion 25, 64, 147–48, 166, 172, 175, 180
India 99, 142, 182, 184
individual compass 49–68
Inesta, Delphine 36–37, 59, 60, 78, 104, 113, 133, 188, 194, 201–02
informal champions 132
informal connections 128
informal power 174–76
institutional bias 3, 6, 179
   see also gender bias
integrity 59
international moves 32–34
International Space Station 2
intrinsic motivation 23–24
introductions 110, 112, 123, 124, 125, 126, 127, 146
Italian Stock Exchange 66
iteration 6, 168

Janjuha-Jivraj, Shaheena (Shaheena) 5, 6–7, 33, 87, 110, 117, 127, 132
Jeffers, Susan 75
job-crafting 191, 195, 196
Jobs, Steve 50

Kahneman, Daniel 21, 24
Kane, Aminata 76–77, 116, 174–75
Kathy (Michaels, Kathy) 103–04, 132, 141, 155–56
knowledge sharing 111–12, 134
Lagarde, Christine 97
Lagarde, Sarah de 42–47
laissez-faire leadership 153, 161
lateral (horizontal) organizational structures 10–11, 171
Lauren 28–29
leadership 10, 102
leadership styles 152–54, 161–63
learning 82–83, 98, 103, 105, 143, 159
LEGO Group 19, 23–24
LeSueur, Michelle 34, 52, 188, 203

life changes 121
   see also international moves; maternity (motherhood)
likeability trap 65, 86–87
LinkedIn 56–57, 62, 111, 122
Linklaters 66
listening skills 34, 79, 83, 97, 128, 145, 158–59, 172
Lloyds 37, 87, 94
London Court of International Arbitration 193
loss aversion 24
luck 4, 199–206
Maltesers adverts 63–64
management 10, 185
Marina 20, 156, 188–89, 196–97, 205
Mars 26–28, 63–64
maternal wall bias 35
maternity (motherhood) 35–37, 103–04, 142, 189
   see also parental leave
Mavrinac, Sarah 110
Me Too movement 185
meetings 36, 80–82, 121, 127, 147, 149, 158–59, 163, 172, 203
Melin, Virginie 67, 205
men's club 137
mentors 52–53, 98, 109, 113, 134–36, 141, 149
   see also employee resource groups
meritocracy 148, 174
Merkel, Angela 97
Michaels, Kathy (Kathy) 103–04, 132, 141, 155–56
micro-habits 39–40
microaggressions 184
micromanagement 61
Millennials 57, 58
Millennium Development Goals 25
mindset 200
   entrepreneurial 12, 108, 113, 124, 180, 195–97
   fixed 39
   growth 47, 95, 186
mistakes (failure) 13, 79–82, 93–95, 102–03, 104–05, 187–88
Mohamed, Amina 25–26
Moneysupermarket Group 144
moral compass 60, 77

motherhood (maternity) 35–37,
103–04, 142, 189
motivation 23–24, 52, 53, 94, 98,
157, 163, 188–89, 196
Mourot-Haxaire, Delphine 7–8,
32–33, 36
Mpofu, Joy 125, 137–38
multicultural teams 163–67
multinational corporations (MNCs)
11
Musk, Elon 101

negotiation skills 47, 74, 88
Netflix 30–31, 95
network mapping 118, 123
network size 119–24
networking 80, 107, 109, 110,
113–25, 136, 138–39, 146
see also connections
networking events 111, 124, 125
neurogenesis 22
neuroplasticity (brain plasticity) 22,
44–45, 93

Obaid, Thoraya Ahmed 52–53,
83–84, 157
Obama, Michelle 97
objective setting 52, 94
see also goal setting
O'Brien, Katharine 85, 87–88
Odgers Berndtson Board Practice
73–74
Olaogun, Motunrayo 62
Oliver, Michele 26–28, 63–64
one-to-one meetings 149, 158–59
ones to watch (OTW) 132, 139, 140,
145–47
opinions (of others) 104
optimism 74, 144
Orange 76, 116
organizational culture 24–25, 30–31,
37–38, 58, 60–61, 89, 134,
140
organizational structure 135–36, 167
hierarchical 10–11, 135, 153, 167,
174
horizontal (lateral) 11, 171
vertical 10–11
organizational values 56–57, 61–62

other-oriented perfectionism 40
outsider perspective 162

pandemic, Covid-19 8, 33, 60, 61, 64,
72, 127, 171–72, 182, 192
parental leave 35, 127
participative leadership 153
partnerships 108, 110, 112–13, 124,
134, 160, 166, 205
Parzani, Claudia 66–67
passion 28–29, 46, 66, 192
perfectionism 40–42, 83, 170
performance appraisals 55, 137, 146
personal responsibilities (domestic
responsibilities) 113–14,
179–80
personal success 187
pivoting 192–93, 194
Planckaert, Marie 19–20, 95, 99–100,
168–69, 202
plenary sessions 128
pluralist leadership 166, 175
politeness 78, 87
Population Fund (UN) 52
positive energy 62, 144, 174
power 174–76
Pradhan, Kshama 142–43, 159–60,
164–65
prefrontal cortex 90
preparation 81, 97, 124, 200, 203
priming 24, 90
problem solving 42–44, 45–47, 48
procrastination 162, 171
professional-personal (work-life)
balance 172–73, 196
promotions (career progression) 75–
76, 87–88, 98–99, 136–37,
154, 177–98
see also champions; coaching; glass
cliff positions; mentors;
stretch roles
prospect theory 24
Proudfoot, Devon 29–30
psychological safety 19, 24, 27, 47,
155, 157, 164, 172
Publicover, Jennifer 31–32, 56, 65,
102–03, 123, 186
purpose 8–9, 26–27, 51–55, 56, 62,
63–64, 118, 203

Quader, Naadia 65, 189
question techniques 128

reciprocity 109, 116–17, 118–19, 126, 130, 171
Reed Smith 54–55
reflection 59
regulators 78–79
relationships (human relations) 104, 188
remote (virtual) working 169, 181, 182
resilience 44, 82, 94, 99, 102, 144, 174, 189, 206
rest 197
Rhimes, Shonda 168
rigidity 38–40, 201
risk management 21, 78–79
risk-taking 31, 79, 88, 94, 187–88
roadmaps 51, 56
role models 10, 77–78, 85, 97, 98, 134, 171, 185, 190–95
Rose, Alison 2
Royal Bank of Canada (RBC) 31, 56

salespeople 34, 112
Saudi Arabia 99
saying 'no' 72–73, 74, 85, 86, 87, 89–90, 92
saying 'yes' 73, 74, 85–91
SDGs (Sustainable Development Goals) 25–26, 60, 61
'second shift' responsibilities see personal responsibilities (domestic responsibilities)
Security Council for the Arab League (UN) 25
self-awareness 77, 189
self-efficacy 98–99, 102, 178, 194
self-esteem 99
self-oriented perfectionism 40
servant leadership 152, 153, 166
service 67
sextants 49, 68
Shackleton, Ernest 10
Shaheena (Janjuha-Jivraj) 5, 6–7, 33, 87, 110, 117, 127, 132
Shchuckina, Marina (Marina) 20, 156, 188–89, 196–97, 205

Shearman & Sterling 193
shortcuts 44–45
Shura Council 52, 83
small changes, power of 94
social affirmation 87
social media 10, 119, 121, 126
    see also LinkedIn
social mobility 37–38, 201
socially-prescribed perfectionism 40
soft power 174–76
sponsorship 110, 113, 135
    see also advocacy; champions
stakeholder mapping 145, 150
status homophily 114–15, 120
status quo 65–66
status quo bias 24
STEM fields 149, 191
stereotyping 3, 27, 63, 89, 161, 162
storming stage 165
    see also conflict
storytelling 67, 179
stress 40, 72, 76–77, 99, 205
    see also burnout
stress responses 22
stretch roles 92–96, 105, 145–46
success 99–100, 178–81, 185–90, 203
survival instinct 43
Sustainable Development Goals (SDGs) 25–26, 60, 61
System 1 thinking 21

team building 46, 67, 83, 151–76
    cross-functional 79
    culture 37–38
technology 181–83
testing (experimentation) 66, 78, 79, 103, 168, 179
Thorning-Lund, Susanne 73–74, 162–63, 173, 180–81
Tiara (Cinderella) syndrome 136–37, 142
time management 36
TotalEnergies 19, 95
toxic work culture 60–61
transactional leadership 153, 161–62
transferable skills 34, 96, 194, 195, 196, 197
transformational leadership 153, 161
transparency 52, 59, 63, 104

trust 10, 34, 60–61, 142, 144, 147, 165, 169–73, 176
Twitter 101
'Tyranny of Politeness' (Janjuha-Jivraj) 87

uncertainty 21–22, 24–25, 39, 102, 194
United Nations (UN) 25–26, 52–53, 83
  SDGs 60, 61
  UN High Commissioner for Refugees 66
  UN Women 27, 64
  Unstereotype Alliance 27, 64

Valančiūnas, Jonas 102–03
value homophily 114, 115
values 52, 55–57, 59–69, 87, 114, 115, 143, 179
values alignment 57, 62, 63, 68
Velshi, Rumina 78–79, 149, 171–72, 175, 187–88, 201
Verjee, Nadia 85–86, 204
versatility 159–60
vertical organizational structures 10–11
Vincent Ortiz, Lucie-Claire 80–83, 108–09, 110–12
virtual (remote) working 169, 181, 182

visibility 105, 127, 138, 142, 143, 147
vision 10, 147, 152, 154, 158, 189

Weckstrom, Cecilia 19, 23–24, 71–72, 160, 203–04
well-being 22, 29, 62, 99, 206
Whitney (Gore, Whitney) 30–31, 31–32, 95, 122, 125, 168, 187, 202
Williams, Professor Joan C. 35
Women in STEM Mentoring Programme 149
Women's Economic Forum 181
Women's World Cup 2
Woodham, Karen 61–62, 144–45, 203
Woodhull, Victoria 51
work, future of 181–82
work curfews 155–56
work-life (professional-personal) balance 172–73, 196
working from home 169, 181, 182
World Economic Forum (WEF) 56–57, 62

X 101

Yaccarino, Linda 101
younger employees 37
  see also Gen X; Gen Z; Millennials
Yousafzai, Malala 51

Looking for another book?

Explore our award-winning books from global business experts in General Business

Scan the code to browse

www.koganpage.com/general-business

Also from Kogan Page

ISBN: 9781398600447

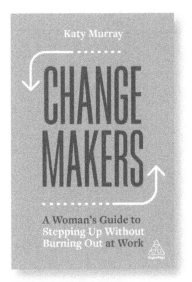

ISBN: 9781398605060

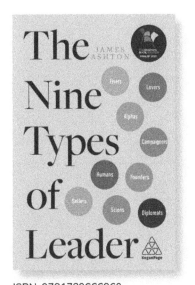

ISBN: 9781789666960

ISBN: 9781789668360

www.koganpage.com